The Ghetto, the Garden, and the Gospel

*What Every Christian Needs to Understand
About Poverty in America*

Joe Ader

RISING
RIVER
MEDIA

Published under license by Rising River Media.
www.risingrivermedia.org

ISBN 13 - 978-0-578-48068-8

Cover design of both print and digital versions by Jonathan Schuler.
Original cover composition by Heath Harmon.
Final cover composition by Lawton Printing, Spokane, WA.

This is a work of non-fiction. Some names have been changed to protect the privacy of those involved.

Books and Study Guides are available at UnderstandingPoverty.com/.
Also available in digital form as an eBook.

Table of Contents

From The Publisher

Author's Preface and Acknowledgments

Introduction

Part 1 - The Ghetto
>How My Journey Got Started (17)
>What Do You Know? (23)
>Mollie, the Mother Of Poverty (33)
>Trading Places (41)
>The Time Is Now (47)
>Understanding Our Differences (57)
>Looking Closer at a Family in Poverty (67)

Part 2 - The Garden
>What Causes Poverty? (79)
>From The Garden To The Ghetto (87)
>The Cause And The Cure (99)

Part 3 - The Gospel
>New Creations (111)
>Contentment In Love (119)
>Seek the Welfare of the City (129)
>An Ambassador, Not A Judge (135)
>The Iron Rule (143)
>Going Upriver (149)
>Tools You Can Use (157)
>From Knowledge to Action (173)

Endnotes

From The Publisher

I met Joe Ader roughly a year after he moved to Spokane. Joe had spent that year working with Family Promise of Spokane to launch "Open Doors," Spokane's first 24/7 emergency shelter for families experiencing homelessness. At the time I was collecting articles from leaders of local homeless service agencies for a book project entitled *30 Days and 30 Ways of Doing Good*. I challenged Joe to write an article about his work with Family Promise and Open Doors. He submitted a great article, *"Through the Eyes of a 9-Year Old,"* which became Day 19 of the finished book. During the intervening months, I had opportunities to attend a couple of Joe's "Understanding Poverty" workshops which he conducted for schools and churches in Spokane. I was impressed and intrigued by Joe's material. Little did I know then that there was more to come. Much more.

Shortly after I published *30 Days and 30 Ways*, Joe approached me with a question: Could I help him turn his Understanding Poverty workshop material into a book? Joe's question and my answer started us both on a six-year-long journey of discovery and collaboration. I discovered the depth of personal experience and of practical and biblical insight Joe brings to the discussion of poverty and how we as Christians should respond to those experiencing it. As someone who had worked among the homeless, the poor and the marginalized for nearly 20 years, I thought I had a fairly good grasp on ministry among the marginalized. But working with Joe to bring his material into print had the unexpected impact of exposing my own blind-spots. I experienced more than one "Aha!" moment as Joe's practical observations and insights brought many of my own experiences among the marginalized into sharper focus, giving me new clarity concerning people and issues. His clear explanation of the differences between the residents of Middle Classburg, America, and Povertyville, USA is worth the price of the book alone. And that's just one reason why every Christian in America should read this book. There's more. Much more. But I'll let you discover that "more" for yourself and experience your own "Aha!" moments.

It isn't very often that a small non-profit publishing house has the opportunity to work with such high-caliber material. As a publisher, I'm both flattered and honored to be able to share Joe's journey and to bring this book into print. It is my genuine pleasure to recommend and to offer you *The Ghetto, the Garden, and the Gospel: What Every Christian in American Needs to Understand About Poverty in America.*

Maurice Smith
Executive Director & Publisher
Rising River Media

Author's Preface and Acknowledgments

I never set out to write a book.

I set out to understand a world that didn't make sense to me-the world of poverty. As a teenager thrust into the chaos of a Los Angeles whorehouse on a "church camp" mission trip, I found myself praying for safety with my back pressed against a wall. That moment-and the indifferent shrug of the children who lived there-started a lifelong journey. It was the first time I realized that what shook me to my core was someone else's normal.

Over the decades, that journey has taken me across the country and around the world. I've worked in inner-city neighborhoods, run nonprofits, started shelters, and sat with the powerful and the powerless alike. But the heart of this book didn't come from boardrooms or budgets-it came from sidewalk conversations, late-night prayers, and the painful beauty of trading places with those living without stable homes, stable jobs, or stable lives.

This book is for every Christian who feels the tension between Sunday sermons and Monday streets. It's for those who believe the Gospel isn't just good news for heaven, but a call to bring hope, dignity, and restoration here and now. It's for the suburban small group that wants to serve, and the urban pastor who wonders if anyone sees their struggle. And it's for anyone ready to lay down assumptions and pick up a deeper compassion.

The Ghetto, the Garden, and the Gospel isn't a policy manual or political argument. It's a mirror, a map, and a mission. A mirror to help us see our own blind spots. A map to trace the spiritual and systemic roots of poverty. And a mission to help us step into the radical love Jesus modeled-one person, one family, one neighborhood at a time.

I invite you to read with curiosity, humility, and courage. Not just to understand the world of poverty, but to ask what your role is in transforming it.

Let's get to work.

Acknowledgments

This book wouldn't exist without a long list of people who have encouraged, challenged, and carried me through the journey of writing it.

First, to my family - Don and Dee Ader, Grant Ader, and Hayes Ader-thank you for your steadfast love and belief in me. Donnie Ader and Constance

Vaverka, you are not only my siblings but also real-life examples of resilience through adversity and poverty.

To my friends - Zac Minton, Arnold Peterson, the Oakley family, and Steve Allen, you've each played a part in keeping me grounded and moving forward, whether you knew it or not.

The children and families we serve at Family Promise of Spokane are my daily inspiration. Your stories are the heartbeat of this book and the reason I fight so hard to get this message out.

To Maurice Smith - this book would still be a "someday" project if not for you. Your constant encouragement and accountability have been invaluable. You never stopped nudging me forward, and I'm grateful you didn't.

A special thanks to my early readers and idea-sharers: Ryan Oelrich, Chili Lugo Peña, Jim Burke, Barry Barfield, Jamie Hipp, Blake Chilton, and Emma Hughes. Emma, you've done more than your fair share. Your ability to take my visionary ideas and put them into practice has been invaluable. The way you oversee day-to-day operations at Family Promise of Spokane gave me the space to finish what I started with this book.

I'm deeply grateful to Ruby Payne, Steve Corbett, Brian Fikkert, and the Notre Dame Lab for Economic Opportunity for building the foundation on which this book stands.

To Matt Smith at PepsiCo - thank you for being the first to invite me to train Frito-Lay executives. That one moment helped me realize that these concepts apply to both businesses and churches.

To Rachel and Jason Thurman - thank you for connecting me to PayPal and for your constant encouragement.

To Matt Chandler and The Village Church - thank you for giving me the space to try out-of-the-box things, including teaching this material to your church members first.

The resources that informed this work are too many to list, but a few standouts are: *A Framework for Understanding Poverty*, *Bridges Out of Poverty*, *Building a People of Power*, and of course, the ESV Bible. I truly have stood on the shoulders of giants in this work. A special shoutout to Ruby Payne, who was the first to tell me I should write this book.

Author's Preface

My family has made countless sacrifices-weekends, early mornings, and missed evenings-so I could write, train, and teach. Thank you for your patience and love. And a nod to the Panera Bread in Spokane Valley, where many of these ideas came to life over breakfast.

To the woman who shared her story with me and asked to remain anonymous-thank you for your courage and trust. Your story matters. It helped reshape how I think about children in poverty and gave me tools to better serve others.

This book is not just a collection of thoughts - it's part of a larger mission. My faith in Jesus Christ, and His call to care for the poor, has shaped every word. The concepts here are lived out every day by the team at Family Promise of Spokane. To the staff - your commitment has made this more than theory. As I write this, you have rehoused more families than any other organization in our region-possibly the country. That's what impact looks like. Well done.

Finally, to the 3,000+ families who have faced the trauma of homelessness and allowed me to walk with you-you've validated the concepts in this book and taught me what no textbook ever could.

If I've forgotten anyone, please know that your presence in my life matters deeply. I am grateful beyond words.

Joe Ader
Spokane, WA

The Ghetto, the Garden and the Gospel

Introduction

Right Now

Right now, in cities and towns across America, scenes unfold that paint a vivid picture of the immediacy of our modern crises and echos the stories of Christian's ancient past. Right now in America, a teenage mother, caught in the grip of poverty, is birthing a child into homelessness. Right now in America, a refugee fleeing persecution steps onto a new land uncertain of what their future will hold. Right now, a gang of young men is walking the streets rabble-rousing and will soon be a problem for the authorities.

These stories of struggle and resilience are not mere stories of our times, but they are echos of stories deeply entwined with the fabric of our Christian faith. They echo the humble beginnings of a 1st Century man named Jesus; who was born into homelessness to a teenage mother, who spent time as a refugee fleeing persecution, who, along with a group of young men, found himself in trouble with the authorities. Jesus lived a life on earth that reflects the lives of the poor in our communities today. But the question for you to discover is "Why?"

Why Should Every Christian Read This Book?

The answer is quite simple: *Because the poor matter to Jesus.* Whatever matters to Jesus should matter to us. Not only that, but according to Jesus, how we serve the poor has eternal consequences. Let me say that again. How we serve the poor has eternal consequences!

Jesus' life on earth was marked by poverty, including finding himself homeless and without a place to lay his head on both the day of his birth and his last night before his imprisonment and eventual crucifixion. As profound as that is to think about, what he says in Matthew 25: 31-46 should shake every Christian to their very core and cause deep introspection of how each one of us cares for the poor.

At the close of his last day of freedom and ministry on earth, Jesus explains that at the end of the age God will judge "all the nations" by separating every person into two groups which he describes as sheep and goats. He will invite the sheep to "inherit the kingdom prepared for you from the foundation of the world" (Matthew 25:34). But He will command the goats, "Depart from me, you cursed, into the eternal fire prepared for the devil and his angels" (Matthew

25:41).

So what is this talking about and what is the defining characteristic that is so important that it distinguishes the sheep (believers) who will inherit the kingdom from the goats (unbelievers) who will be cast into the fire for eternity? The answer is how they cared for the poor and the marginalized.

> "For I was hungry and you gave me food, I was thirsty and you gave me drink, I was a stranger and you welcomed me, I was naked and you clothed me, I was sick and you visited me, I was in prison and you came to me."

Jesus' message is hard to miss, although many people do. While we wait for His return, the calling of every believer is to serve the poor and the marginalized -- people Jesus collectively referred to as "the least of these." And we're to serve them as if we're serving Jesus Himself. So, let me ask you the really difficult question: Today, if God were to judge the genuineness of your faith by how you served "the least of these," where would you spend eternity?

> If God were to judge the genuineness of your faith by how you served "the least of these," where would you spend eternity?

This is why you need to read this book: because these things really do matter to Jesus, and they need to matter to us. The goal of this book is to inspire, equip, and motivate you to better serve the "least of these" and all who Jesus loves.

A Journey Into Understanding Poverty

Welcome to our journey into better understanding poverty: both its causes and its ripple effects. Our approach on this journey will be specifically biblical, as opposed to sociological or even economical, although we will explore both social and economic issues. Together we'll discover a garden that was lost, a ghetto that was created, a gospel that needs to be proclaimed, and a Kingdom that is coming. We'll also discover how poverty is about broken relationships, and a profound tear in the social fabric of God's creation. That tear and those broken relationships impact each and every one of us, regardless of our

Introduction

socio-economic status. Those relationships were broken, and the fabric of God's creation was torn, in the Garden of Genesis 3. The result of those events wasn't simply that the man and woman were expelled from the Garden. That's true, but it was much worse than that. They were also cast into a worldwide ghetto of their own creation. Sometimes, the worst thing God can do is to allow us to experience the full consequences of our choices. But, more about that later.

Our journey through this book is best understood in three parts. Part One is about understanding a reality that we're calling the Ghetto. The term ghetto originated in Venice, Italy, in the 1500s, to describe the Jewish area of the City, taking its name from a nearby foundry (ghetto is the Venetian word for "foundry"). By the late 19th Century, the term ghetto was being commonly used to refer to crowded urban quarters where members of various minority groups lived, usually due to social, legal, or economic pressures.

But the strongest and darkest ghetto in all of man's history is not social, legal, racial, ethnic or economic. It's spiritual. It's the ghetto that the man and woman found themselves in following their expulsion from the Garden. This spiritual ghetto knows no ethnic, racial, economic, or geographic boundaries. It's everywhere, and it touches each and every one of us, until we're set free from it in Christ. Its distinguishing characteristics include disparities, injustice, poverty and much more. On our journey through the Ghetto we'll take a look at government attempts to define and address these characteristics. We will meet some of its residents: people who live in Middle Classburg, America and Povertyville, USA. We'll work to understand their worldviews and how they cope with their daily living conditions in the Ghetto.

> The strongest and darkest ghetto in all of man's history is not social, legal, racial, ethnic or economic; it's spiritual.

Part Two of our journey will take us on a walk through the Garden. Why? Because our expulsion from the Garden explains our life in the Ghetto. But understanding the how's and why's will require us to look at the most commonly offered causes for the Ghetto, explain why those suggested causes are helpful, but not sufficient, and then look at the biblical causes of poverty -- all of which had their beginning in the Garden.

Part Three of our journey will take us into the biblical cure for the Ghetto and all of its related ripple effects -- the Gospel. Along the way we'll discover the good news of what God has done to restore our broken relationships and to heal and mend the torn social fabric of His creation. We'll discover our new and amazing calling to bring the good news of His reconciliation and the promise of His restoration to the those still trapped in the Ghetto. And as our journey concludes, we'll discover how our calling translates into lives of sacrificial service on behalf of the poor, the hungry, the naked, the stranger, the prisoner and the marginalized -- those whom Jesus collectively called, "the least of these."

Part 1 - The Ghetto

The term *ghetto* originated in Venice, Italy, in the 1500s, to describe the Jewish area of the City, taking its name from a nearby foundry (*ghetto* is the Venetian word for "foundry"). By the late 19th Century, the term *ghetto* was being commonly used to refer to crowded urban quarters where members of various minority groups lived, usually due to social, legal, or economic pressures.

The Ghetto, the Garden and the Gospel

How My Journey Got Started

"Get wisdom; get insight; don't forget, and don't turn away from the words of my mouth. Do not forsake her, and she will keep you; love her, and she will guard you." (Proverbs 4:5-6)

The Night That Started It All

Knock, knock, knock!

The sound made me pop up out of bed. I heard it again: knock, knock, knock! My heart was racing now as I looked around. Through the dim post-midnight light, I could make out the silhouette of the other teenage boy in the room. Like me, my roommate was sitting up on his wireframe bed, startled by the knocking sound.

KNOCK, KNOCK, KNOCK! The knock had become a fist, pounding on the door. "Who is it?" I squeaked, in a whispered voice that had the tell tale signs of puberty . . . and fear! More fist pounding. KNOCK, KNOCK, KNOCK.

"Come on baby! Let me in! I'm not drunk!" a man's voice called out from the other side of the door. "You, have the wrong room!" I said a little louder this time. BOOM, BOOM. "Let me in B**ch!" he screamed from the hallway.

The time for talk was over. Hearts racing and adrenaline pumping at full steam, my roommate and I pushed our wireframe beds up against the door, huddled together in the corner, and began to pray. I wasn't experienced at prayer, but at this particular moment it didn't matter. It wasn't an eloquent prayer -- just a desperate one "Dear God, Help!" At 5'2" and 86lbs, I knew that my 13 year old body didn't stand a chance of defending myself if this man came through the door.

BOOM! Now the fist had become a foot. He kicked the door so hard that, for a split second, the door bowed inward and we could see the shoe of the man's kicking foot. "Dear God, help!" I prayed more fervently, thinking to myself, "How did I end up trapped in a room in a whorehouse in inner-city Los Angeles in the first place?"

The Ghetto, the Garden and the Gospel

Not Your Typical Church Camp

"Come with us to camp next week," said the youth pastor, when I visited his Wednesday night group for the first time. Like most teenage boys who attend church without being forced to by their parents, I was there for the cute girl that invited me and not for God. "Sure," I told him, expecting camp to be in the mountains somewhere. It might be fun to run around in the woods, I thought, play some games, have a bonfire, and watch everyone get worked into a tearful frenzy on Thursday night as the camp's hired gun speaker along with a singer on an acoustic guitar issue repeated invitations to accept Jesus into your heart. You know, the typical church camp experience. And besides that, there will be cute girls there.

The next Saturday I was already in the van on our way to camp when I realized that camp was not going to be in the mountains or the woods. Camp was going to be in a five story brick building in inner-city Los Angeles, where we would be staying with prostitutes and their children for a week. That was an unexpected surprise for sure. Now, here I was, in the middle of the night with a man trying to break down the door of our third floor room. No fire escape, no phone, the youth pastor and other students were in rooms at the other end of the hall. There was no way out.

"God, help! Help us!"

Just then, a big voice came from somewhere down the corridor. For two frightened junior-high kids, it sounded like the voice of an angel, although I doubt God allows the angels to use that kind of vocabulary, "HEY, YOU ARE ON THE WRONG F****ING FLOOR! GET THE F*** OUT OF HERE," shouted the almost-angelic voice at the man pounding on our door.

It worked. We could hear the man stumble away from the door, down the hallway, and up the stairs. And just like that, it was over.

My roommate and I gathered the beds up and spent the rest of the night somewhere between a state of fear and excitement. I couldn't wait to tell the kids what had happened. So, when the next morning came, I went downstairs and did just that. I told the kids who lived in the building the whole night's adventure. As I got to the climax of the story, the looks on their faces left me crestfallen: boredom. They shrugged their shoulders and simply said, "So what?"

How My Journey Got Started

That was it. That was the moment when I was struck with a new realization that would drive me into study and eventually a career. That was the moment I realized that these kids, even though they were my same age, had lives so different from mine. What I had experienced that night is everyday life for them. That man could have been one of their dads. As a result, they saw the world and everything in it differently than I did. After that moment, and for the rest of the week, I intently watched the kids that lived in the building play and interact. I watched in shock and terror as they raced shopping carts with kids sitting in them down the hill into LA traffic. In over-protective middle class Orange County, California, where I grew up, most parents made their kids wear a helmet and shoulder pads just to ride bikes on the sidewalk in front of their house! Compared to my normal environment, this place was like a foreign land. It left me wondering, "Why? How did this happen? Why is it like this?" That started my journey of trying to research and understand poverty.

At that time, research on poverty and its roots was not so easy to do. The internet only existed at research institutes and nobody had heard of it yet. Google was about as far-fetched an idea as time-travel. I actually had to go to a library to do research. So, off to the library I went and started searching for books that talked about the subject of poverty.

Later that summer, I visited Saddleback Church again, the same youth group which had taken me to "camp" earlier that year. This time though, the youth pastor I had originally met had been replaced. While I can't definitely say why he had lost his job, something tells me that taking a group of middle schoolers to an hourly motel and calling it "camp" might have had something to do with it. His interim replacement was a mountain of a man named Steve Rutenbar. Steve would later lead Saddleback's Missions and Disaster Relief efforts around the world, but at this time he was just a dad, filling in because the youth were without a pastor. However, God would use Steve that night to share the good news about Jesus Christ with me and it resonated with me. God invaded the depths of the soul of an abused and angry teenager and revealed his light. From that moment on, both my faith journey and my journey into understanding poverty have been intricately woven together.

The historic timing of all of this was fitting because while I had an interest in understanding poverty, honestly, books about poverty were hard to find at my school and the public library in South Orange County. Then, all of a sudden, the events of the time overtook my research. The beating of Rodney King and the LA riots that followed in 1992 focused attention on the issue of inner-city poverty. Suddenly, a lot was being written about poverty. In addition to that, my community was beginning to see gangs and gang violence for the first time. One of my classmates was shot in a drive-by shooting after school and we later found out it was planned by another friend of mine. Up to that point the kids we knew who were in gangs were all want-a-be gangsters, but things became very real, very fast. Many of these kids were first generation Americans who had grown up in poverty and their parents had moved them to South Orange County to avoid these types of issues. However, as I would later discover, the issues were as much internal as they were external. You can't move away and expect things to just be different. Our struggles are hardwired within us. When we move, so do our issues.

More Steps into Understanding Poverty

My journey eventually led me to Baylor University in Waco, Texas. Like many college freshmen, I was required to do community service hours for my sociology class. I honestly didn't want to do it. I was looking for the easiest way to meet the requirement when I heard that Habitat for Humanity was having a weekend conference at a rival school (which shall remain unnamed, but I'll call it Aggieland). Being a clever undergrad, I thought to myself, I can go to the conference, get all my hours done in one weekend, and never have to do community service again! Perfect! It was a brilliant plan, or so I thought. But down at Aggieland, I met the founder of Habitat for Humanity and fell in love with the organization. So, for the next two years, I became the President of Habitat for Humanity at Baylor in Waco. My brilliant attempt to get out of community service resulted in over 4,000 hours of community service.

Through that experience, the Lord started teaching me some things: things that were good, things that just didn't make a lot of sense, and things that rubbed on me the wrong way. I would later bring many of those lessons with me into ministry at the Village Church in Flower Mound, Texas. While on staff as the Local Missions Pastor at The Village, I oversaw some mission teams both in South Dallas and in Guatemala. They had run into some problems that could have resulted in serious harm to the team members. As we worked through both situations, I realized that our teams were made up of middle class people who had good hearts and genuine desires to serve. But they had no understanding of the communities they were serving and how poverty had impacted the mindsets of those living in those communities. As a result, our teams didn't understand the neighborhoods that they were working in or what was going on around them. That's when I decided to start teaching our people about poverty.

Originally, I started teaching a lot of what was written by Ruby Payne, in her book *Framework for Understanding Poverty*.[1] After teaching through Ruby Payne's material several times, I realized that, while it was good at explaining the current state of those living in poverty, it didn't say anything about where poverty comes from or what we should do about it. So, that's really what I've spent more than fourteen years working on. That's what the meat of this book is about. What does poverty look like? Where does it come from? What should we as Christians do about it?

My journey has brought me all over the country and to parts of Latin America. It has put me both on stages in front of government officials and CEOs of major corporations, and on the street talking with people experiencing homelessness, often on the same day. I have had the good fortune to run community gardens, food banks, counseling centers, to create nonprofit resource centers, and to create homeless shelters. I have influenced a corporation to feed millions of hungry children. Also, I have been able to oversee an organizations that has rehoused thousands of families with children out of homelessness. Lastly, I have gotten to experience the truly life-changing work of serving those who are like Christ.

Now, take a deep breath and have an open and curious mind as you seek to understand poverty, just as I am. Let's get started.

Reflecting and Looking Ahead

1. In this chapter, the author shared about why he got involved in the issue of poverty. As we start this journey together, it's important for you to discover your "why?" and your personal motivation for exploring this topic. How has your own life been impacted by poverty and related issues, such as homelessness? Explain.

2. Think of someone in your life who modeled service to the poor, someone you would like to emulate. Describe them and how they impacted you.

3. What do you hope or expect to learn from this book?

For Additional Study

For additional individual or group study, including a more in-depth look at what Scripture teaches on this topic, see the Study Guide for this book.

What Do You Know?

"Judge not, that you be not judged. For with the judgment you pronounce you will be judged, and with the measure you use it will be measured to you. Why do you see the speck that is in your brother's eye, but don't notice the log that is in your own eye? Or how can you say to your brother, 'Let me take the speck out of your eye,' when there is the log in your own eye? You hypocrite, first take the log out of your own eye, and then you will see clearly to take the speck out of your brother's eye." (Matthew 7:1-5)

Understanding Ourselves (to Understand Others)

If you and I are to truly understand poverty and the people whose daily lives are caught up in it, we need to begin with a better understanding of ourselves and our own perspectives. The journey into understanding poverty is also a journey into understanding ourselves. Our journey into understanding poverty is also a journey of self-discovery --

> The journey into understanding poverty is also a journey into understanding ourselves.

discovering who we are, how we view the world, and why we treat others the way we do. In the above passage from the Gospel of Matthew, Jesus describes this journey of self-discovery in terms of a personal challenge, the challenge of dealing with the "log" in our own eye, which skews our perspective, before we examine the "speck" in someone else's eye. While poverty is certainly more than a speck, the log in our own eye renders us blind and unable to see the reality of poverty, how it impacts the daily lives of those bound up in it, and, most importantly, how to respond in ways that are both compassionate and productive. So, let's take a few minutes to do some personal introspection.

In my Understanding Poverty workshops, I ask all of the participants to do a survey entitled "What Do You Know?"[2] The survey is designed to help everyone better identify the "log" in their eye, so to speak. I've reproduced the survey below. As you'll see on the following page, it's divided into three sections or categories: Poverty, Middle Class, and Wealth, with self-identifying statements under each category. Got it?

What Do You Know? (A Survey)[3]
Under each category, circle any statements which apply to you

What Do You Know About Poverty?
1. I know which sections of town have the best yard sales.
2. I know how to get someone out of jail.
3. I know how to fight and defend myself physically.
4. I know which buses to take to get where I need to go.
5. I know how to keep my clothes from being stolen at the Laundromat.
6. I know how to live without electricity and a phone.

What Do You Know About Middle Class?
1. I know how to get my children into Little League, piano lessons, soccer, etc.
2. I know how to order in a nice restaurant.
3. I know how to use a credit card, checking account, and savings account
4. I know how to talk to my children about going to college.
5. I know how to get insurance.
6. I know a repair service to call when items break.

What Do You Know About Wealth?
1. I know how to read a menu in French, English, and another language.
2. I know and have favorite restaurants in different countries of the world.
3. I know how to hire a decorator to identify the appropriate themes and items with which to decorate the house for the holidays.
4. I know how to staff and maintain multiple residences.
5. I know how to schedule a private plane.
6. I know how to enroll my children in the preferred private school.

If you haven't done so yet, it's your turn to take the survey. Look at the three categories. If you can say "yes" to a statement, circle it. Do this for each category, working your way all the way down the list. Don't skip anything. And, yes, it's an exaggerated survey, but there's a point behind it.

Once you're done, here's what you need to do next. Look at your survey results. Of the three categories (Poverty, Middle Class, Wealth), which category has the most circled statements in it? Circle that category title (if you have a tie, circle both) and remember it. While the survey is exaggerated, it serves the purpose of giving you an idea of your background and the perspective you bring to any discussion of understanding poverty.

What I have discovered after doing this exercise at hundreds of workshops over the years is that the vast majority of the people in the room have self-categorized as middle class. In fact, in over a hundred workshops I've done, I've had only six people self-categorize as wealthy.

Here's my point. It tends to be predominantly middle class Christians who attend these workshops -- people with limited experience with or understanding of genuine poverty. This exercise highlights the reality that you and I must first understand who we are and where we're coming from before we can truly see and understand poverty from a different perspective. We'll talk about what it means for those of us who are middle class to "trade places" with those living in poverty later in chapter 4.

Alright, take a scrap piece of paper and write the category (Poverty, Middle Class or Wealth) that you have the most circled under. Now, take that piece of paper, crumple it up, and throw it away! Yes, throw it away! This simple act symbolizes our need to lay down our own resources and pre-conceptions and embrace new thoughts and ideas of how others might view the world. Each of us needs to make a genuine effort to see life and poverty from a new perspective. It's time to "throw away" what we thought we knew about poverty, because sometimes the greatest obstacle we must overcome is what we think we know.

> It's time to "throw away" what we thought we knew about poverty.

Three Types of Poverty

Now that you and I have discovered who we are (i.e., the perspective that guides our thinking) and have symbolically discarded our old perspective, it's time to take a fresh look at life, poverty, and the people for whom poverty isn't a survey category, but a life experience. I want us to begin by better understanding the three basic categories of poverty: Situational Poverty, Generational Poverty, and Extreme Poverty.

Situational Poverty

Situational Poverty is a sudden change in our financial position that results in being thrust into poverty for a season. It's like this. I had a job, but for whatever reason, I lost my job, and I'm temporarily thrust into poverty. I'm in a state of poverty temporarily, until I get another job.

> Situational poverty is a sudden change in our financial position that results in being thrust into poverty for a season.

But, through the experience, my mindset and the way I view the world stays consistent with more of a Middle Class viewpoint. Once I get a job again income starts coming in I quickly move out of the state of poverty. However, some instances of situational poverty do result in a long term state of poverty. You will often see this happen with illness. For example you will see someone who has been living in Middle Class their whole life, but an illness comes and the medical costs thrust them into poverty. For some, particularly seniors, their financial situation may not ever improve so they are living in poverty the remainder of their days, but their mindset still more aligns with a middle class way of thinking. We will explore the differences in middle class and poverty ways of thinking later.

Generational Poverty

Generational Poverty is different from Situational Poverty. It isn't a temporary situation. Generational Poverty is a state of poverty that usually lasts lifetimes from generation to generation. For example, when you speak with someone whose background is Generational Poverty, you

> Generational Poverty is a state of poverty that usually lasts a whole lifetime and from generation to generation.

might hear them say something like: "My grandmother was poor her whole life, my mother was poor her whole life, and I'm probably going to be poor my whole life." Generational Poverty is the most common type of poverty and therefore most of this book will focus on this type of poverty.

Extreme Poverty

Extreme Poverty means you're earning less than $1.90 per day.[4] Extreme Poverty is very different from either Situational Poverty or Generational Poverty. In Extreme Poverty, your mindset doesn't matter, because you're

> Extreme Poverty means you're earning less than $1.90 per day.

experiencing such a lack of resources that you're living at subsistence level, and you're simply trying to survive. The good news is that we've made enormous strides worldwide at reducing this kind of poverty. In 1981, the Extreme Poverty rate around the globe stood at 43.8 percent of the world's population. By 2018, it had fallen to 8.8 percent. Unfortunately, the COVID-19 pandemic resulted in a noticeable rise in the extreme poverty rate, from 8.8 percent in 2018 to 9.7 percent in 2020. As of 2022, the most recent year for which complete data is available, that percentage had fallen to 9.7 percent.[5] So, yes, we've made huge strides which you don't often hear about, and that's good news for the globe. But from 1990 to 2020, the total number of Americans experiencing poverty rose by 26.2% as seen in the table below.[6]

While Situational and Extreme Poverty are important, for the remainder of

	1990	2020	Increase/ Decrease
U.S. Population	248,709,873	331,449,281	+33.3%
U.S. Total Poverty	32,580,993 13.1% of Population	41,099,710 12.4% of Population	+26.2%
U.S. Extreme Poverty	1,243,549 3.8% of Total Poverty	828,623 2.0% of Total Poverty	-33.4%
Extreme Poverty Fell by 33.4% From 1990 to 2020 But *Total Poverty Rose* by 26.2% From 1990 to 2020			

this book, we will focus our attention on Generational Poverty in America. And we'll start our exploration with a question: Is poverty relative?

Relative Poverty

As we begin our journey into understanding generational poverty, one of the first things we discover is that poverty is actually relative by location. Let me explain by posing a question, the answer to which may be fairly obvious.

If you've ever moved from one part of the country to another, you'll quickly see what I mean. If you make $55,000 a year and you live in a moderate size city in the central part of the U.S., what socio-economic category are you probably in? Poverty? Middle Class? Wealthy? Answer: Middle Class, of course! But, if you make $55,000 a year and you live in Manhattan, New York, what's your socio-economic category? Answer: probably lower Middle Class, maybe even poverty! Finally, if you make $55,000 a year and you live in South Sudan, Africa, what's your socio-economic category now? Congratulations! You're wealthy! So, yes, poverty really is relative by location.

In addition to being relative by location, poverty is also relative by time. For example, the first home my parents lived in, in the late 50s, could have been purchased new for less than $16,000 (no, that isn't a typo!). To purchase that same exact home today in Southern California it will cost you more than $843,000! Poverty is relative by both time and location.

Therefore, if poverty is relative by both location and time, any monetary definition of poverty which tries to boil poverty down to a person or family making less than a certain number of dollars will not be accurate. Poverty is a moving target.

Poverty is also a universal phenomenon. It occurs everywhere in the world. Every country, every demographic, and every ethnicity experiences poverty. There are contributing factors which result in a higher prevalence of poverty. Rates of poverty differ by race and by gender. For example, in the United States, married Hispanics are about three times more likely to experience poverty than married Caucasian couples, while single African-Americans are twice as likely to experience poverty as Caucasians. So why do we see such differences and disparities with different racial groups? Some of that disparity leads back to government policies, such as *redlining*, that were designed to prevent investment in minority communities. So, yes, such things are important factors affecting poverty, and universities offer entire curriculums on just the topics of race and gender and their relation to poverty. For our purposes, we will focus on foundational trends that we see across poverty, and we'll leave race and gender for future book topics. However, I do want to acknowledge that these are important factors that contribute to poverty. One of those important factors that haunts our history was *redlining*.

What Was Redlining?

From the 1920s through the 1960s, the Federal Government implemented a mapping program to inform mortgage lenders and insurers of which areas of different cities were safe to invest in and which areas were "hazardous." The graphic on this page shows the original map that redlined Spokane, Washington in the 1920's, declaring "*...the proximity to the largest Negro population in the city precludes a higher grading.*"

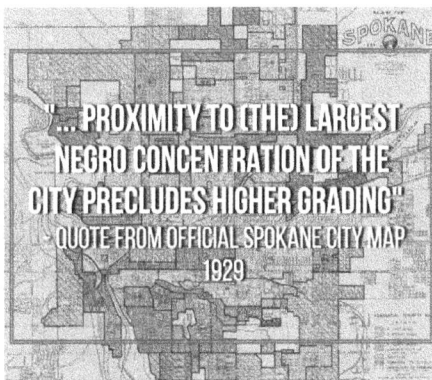

1929 Spokane City Map Showing "Redlining"

The practice of redlining is used today to identify "hazardous" areas such as flood or earthquake zones where investing, making loans, or underwriting insurance could face higher risks. But in prior generations (i.e., the 1920s through the 1960s), one of the main factors used to determine if an area was "less desirable" or "hazardous" was the mere presence of Black individuals in that area. The areas where they were present were marked with a red line

"Redlining" In Your Community?
Use the link below to find your community on a "redline" map and read what they said about your neighborhood then.
https://dsl.richmond.edu/panorama/redlining/

and the policy became known as *redlining*. The ramifications of this policy meant that areas of cities where minorities were present were not invested in and therefore have not seen the same economic growth as other areas. In most US cities you can still see the impact of those policies today.

Migrating Poverty

One important trend to understand is that poverty in America is migrating. From the late 1800s, all the way through the year 2000, poverty in the United States migrated from rural to urban. This move represented a profound change in the American demographic. As families moved off the farms and into the urban centers looking for work and prosperity, it changed the way our communities functioned. Today, we're seeing a similar migration that will have major impacts on how we see and deal with poverty for years to come. Starting around the year 2000, poverty began moving again, this time from urban to suburban, and dramatically changed the demographic landscapes of our cities.

Consider the two maps of Dallas, Texas on the facing page. The map on the

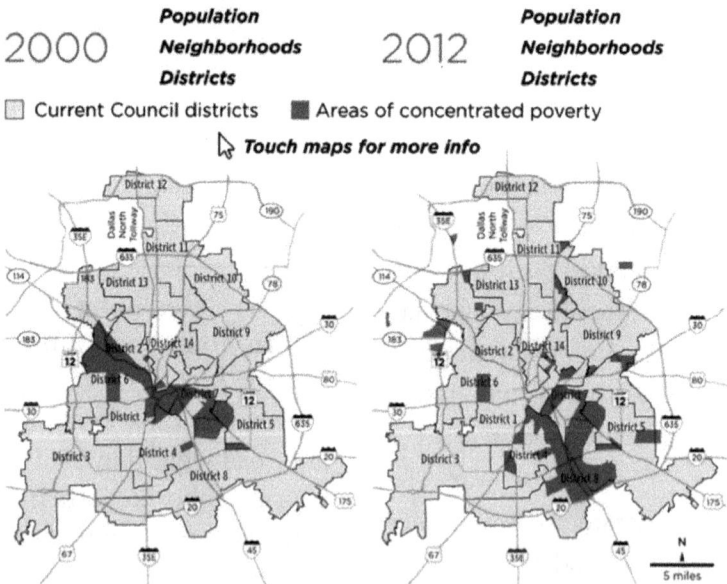

SOURCE: City of Dallas; U.S. Department of Commerce; U.S. Census Bureau   Michael Hogue/Staff Artist

left shows the demographic of poverty in Dallas in the year 2000. Notice how there is a concentration of poverty in the urban core. The map on the right shows how the demographic of poverty in Dallas had changed by 2012. These two identical maps demonstrate the explosive migration of poverty from urban Dallas into suburban Dallas.[7]

A similar migration is happening in every major city in our country. In a now well-known process called gentrification, the urban cores of our cities are being renovated, quickly becoming the cool and chic places to live.[8] They are also becoming the expensive places to live. As a result, gentrification is pushing poverty out of the urban-city cores. People who formerly lived in those neighborhoods are being pushed out. What used to be single-family, low-income neighborhoods are being bought up by developers, knocked down, and replaced with high-density, upper Middle Class condominiums.

The net result of migration and gentrification has been to push people and poverty out of the urban core and into the suburbs. Gone is the Middle Class idea that if we flee to the suburbs, we won't have to look at or address any of these poverty-related issues. That simply isn't true anymore (if it ever was). Nearly every suburban school now has kids and families experiencing homelessness. Nearly every suburban neighborhood now experiences varying densities of genuine poverty (and its ripple effects). And these issues are going to continue for the foreseeable future. The question you and I must answer is whether or not you and I are prepared to face these realities and to bring our biblical faith to bear in meaningful and practical responses.

Reflecting and Looking Ahead

1. Reflecting on this chapter, what did you learn about poverty, and yourself, that you didn't know before?

2. What did you learn from the "What You Know?" survey about your own economic situation? Were you surprised by what you discovered? Explain.

3. Reflecting on the three types of poverty (Situational, Generational, and Extreme), how have you personally witnessed or experienced them? How did it affect you? Explain.

For Additional Study

For additional individual or group study, including a more in-depth look at what Scripture teaches on this topic, see the Study Guide for this book.

3

Mollie, the Mother Of Poverty

And the king of Israel answered, "Tell him, 'Let not him who straps on his armor boast himself as he who takes it off.'" (1 Kings 20:11)

King Ben-hadad of Syria was supremely confident as he prepared to wage war against King Ahab of Israel. Surrounded and supported by thirty-two vassal kings and their armies, Ben-hadad looked invincible. King Ahab was nervous but defiant. "Save your bragging 'til after you've won the battle," Ahab told Ben-hadad. That's good advice. Invincibility soon turned to defeat. King Ahab and Israel won the battle that day, and King Ben-Hadad of Syria learned a painful lesson about unanticipated consequences, along with the limits of his own pride.

If you're familiar with the law of unanticipated consequences, you should probably thank Robert K. Merton, an American sociologist from Columbia University. No, he didn't invent the law, but in 1936 he published an essay, "The Unanticipated Consequences of Social Action," which popularized the notion of unanticipated consequences.[9] In the annals of American Sociology, Merton formalized something we all knew to be true: our actions tend to have both intended and unintended consequences. The intended consequences are the results we were hoping for when we started; the unintended consequences are the results we feared could happen, or the ones we never imagined possible (either positive or negative).

What does this have to do with our discussion of poverty and America's War on Poverty that we're about to look at? Simple. We're about to enter the world of unintended consequences where politicians, generals, policy makers, and people with good intentions should proceed with care. America's War on Poverty would become a textbook example of Professor Merton's observations, with numerous instances both of notable successes, as well as unanticipated and unintended consequences. Just ask Mollie Orshansky.

The President and Poverty

It was November 22nd, 1963 and the young President John F. Kennedy's motorcade was weaving it's way through the streets of Dallas Texas when shots rang out. Within hours President Kennedy was declared deceased and and Vice-President Lyndon Baines Johnson was sworn in as President of the United States. Less than two months later, President Johnson would give his first State of the Union address and in the speech we would declare, "This administration today here and now declares unconditional war on poverty in America."[10]

There was just one minor problem. Up to the moment of that speech, the United States Government had never defined *poverty*. That's right. President Johnson had just declared war against an enemy -- poverty -- that no administration had ever defined. This reality quickly led the Johnson Administration to ask the inevitable question: How do we define poverty to know if we're winning the war? Enter Mollie Orshansky.

Mollie Orshansky, the "Mother of Poverty"

Mollie Orshansky

My guess would be that you've never heard of Mollie Orshansky. That's okay. Whether you recognize her or not, your life as an American has been influenced by Mollie. "How so?" you may ask. Have you ever had a job where you received a paycheck with a line-item deduction for something called "FICA" and another line-item deduction for something called "Medicare." Mollie influenced where that money goes and how it gets spent. Back in 1963, Mollie was working for the Social Security Administration when she read a report by the Department of Agriculture about the minimum amount of food families of different sizes needed to survive. She read another report which argued how a family spends about three times what they spend on food on everything else. Having worked as a statistician, Mollie quickly created an equation which stated that the cost of food for any family size multiplied by three equals the *poverty threshold* for that sized family in America (Food Cost X 3 = Poverty Threshold). Mollie wrote a paper about her "poverty equation," and that was that (or so she thought). Let the unintended consequences begin.[11]

Around six months after Mollie created her "poverty equation" the Johnson administration would make it the official government definition of poverty in America. And that's how the now-famous Federal Poverty Level (FPL), which is quoted on nightly news stations, in newspapers and blogs on a daily basis, came into being, and consequently how Mollie Orshansky became known as the "Mother of Poverty."

Beginning with President Johnson's declaration of a War on Poverty, political events moved quickly. The Economic Opportunity Act of 1964 (August, 1964) created two community action programs: Job Corps and VISTA (Volunteers In Service To America). Next came the Food Stamp Act of 1964 (August 1964). Eight months after that came the Elementary and Secondary Education Act (April, 1965), which created the Head Start Program. And three months after that, the Social Security Amendments Act of 1965 was passed (July, 1965), creating Medicare and Medicaid. So, in a period of just under two years, the American government, under the Johnson Administration, created all of these social welfare programs designed to wage a war against poverty, and to build what President Johnson called *The Great Society*. All of these programs are still around today, along with others that have been added in the years since.

Unintended Consequences

Mollie Orshansky's poverty equation has had several important unintended consequences. The first unintended consequence of Mollie's poverty equation has been the creation of an artificial monetary definition of poverty which dramatically understates poverty in most parts of the country. Monetary definitions of poverty simply aren't adequate because they don't take into account everything that contributes to poverty or financial well-being. The practical (and political) impact of this monetary definition has been to reduce any measure of the War on Poverty to the amount of money spent fighting it. If fighting poverty is a war, then dollars are the bullets, and more bullets means eventual victory, or so it would seem. When President Johnson declared his War On Poverty in 1964, the percentage of Americans living in poverty stood at 19% or approximately 36 million people. In 2015, after fifty-one years of "war," the percentage of Americans living in poverty stood at 13.5% or approximately 43.1 million people. Yes, the percentage of the population experiencing poverty

Figure 1.
Number in Poverty and Poverty Rate Using the Official Poverty Measure: 1959 to 2022

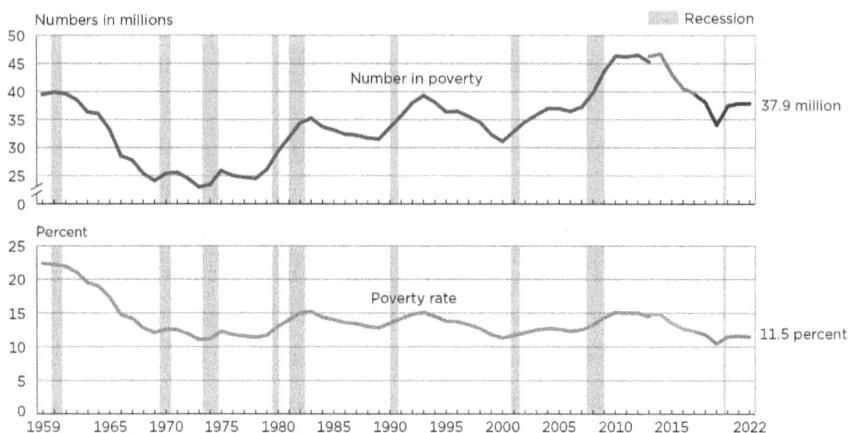

Note: Population as of March of the following year. The data for 2017 and beyond reflect the implementation of an updated processing system. The data for 2013 and beyond reflect the implementation of the redesigned income questions. Refer to Table A-3 for historical footnotes. The data points are placed at the midpoints of the respective years. Information on recessions is available in Appendix C. Information on confidentiality protection, sampling error, nonsampling error, and definitions is available at <https://www2.census.gov/programs-surveys/cps/techdocs/cpsmar23.pdf>.
Source: U.S. Census Bureau, Current Population Survey, 1960 to 2023 Annual Social and Economic Supplements (CPS ASEC).

declined while the gross number of people experiencing poverty rose. The cost of fighting the War on Poverty over those fifty-one years was an estimated $17 trillion.[12] Seven years later, in 2022, after 58 years of "war," those numbers had changed with the number of people experiencing poverty down to 37.9 million or 11% of the population at a total cost about $25 trillion (adjusted for inflation) since 1964 when President Johnson first declared his War on Poverty and launched "the Great Society."[13] But the gross number of people experiencing poverty in 2022 was 1.9 million higher than in 1964 when the War on Poverty was started.

If the first unintended consequence of Mollie's poverty equation was creating a monetary definition of poverty, then the second unintended consequence was creating an artificial standard known as the Federal Poverty Level, or FPL. As of 2025, the FLP for a family of four stood at $32,150, up $950 from 2024. But the widespread adoption and use of the FPL has raised some issues and questions. For example, is that figure really an adequate judge of poverty? And, if not, why not?[14]

I would say, "No, it isn't." Why? The FPL is inadequate - even wrong - for at least two reasons. First, as we learned earlier in chapter 2, poverty is relative by location and by time. Where you live and when you live there can determine whether or not you meet the threshold of the FPL, regardless of income. Second, the FPL is artificial and inadequate because it doesn't account for changes in the real-world costs of such things as housing, medical care, transportation, utilities, and more. Since the creation of the FPL, the cost of everything besides food has increased as a percentage of income. And those unaccounted for increases have

Federal Poverty Level (FPL) For 2024 & 2025		
Family Size	2024 Income	2025 Income
Individual	$15,060	$15,650
Family of 2	$20,440	$21,150
Family of 3	$25,820	$26,650
Family of 4	$31,200	$32,150
Family of 5	$36,580	37,650
Family of 6	$41,960	$43,150
Family of 7	$47,340	$48,650
Family of 8	$52,720	$54,150
Add For Each Additional Person	+ $5,380	+$5,500

unintended consequences. For example, according to the Washington State Department of Commerce, "National research shows a connection between rent increases and homelessness: a $100 increase in rent is associated with an increase in homelessness of between 6 and 32 percent." [15] In fact, 52% of the homeless in the United States exist in just four of the 50 states, California, New York, Florida and Washington State.[16] All of those places have seen astronomical increases in housing costs over the past two decades. Surprisingly, states with high poverty levels and high substance abuse rates, two factors most commonly quoted as causes for homelessness, are actually not near the top in homelessness counts, West Virginia for example.[17]

Such real-world changes, which dramatically impact poverty, are not reflected in the FPL, the U.S. Government continues to use the same poverty equation created by Mollie Orshansky in 1963. Why? Why don't we change what is clearly a bad measure (which poor Mollie never intended to be used for that purpose!)? The answer is simple: politics. Do you want to be in Congress, or to be the President, when the poverty rate doubles durringon your term due to a more realistic calculation? No, no you don't. No politician wants that. Not if they want to get re-elected!

And this brings us to the third unintended consequence of Mollie's poverty equation. In order to make allowances for an unrealistic formula (the FPL), government programs began creating new and convoluted formulas to qualify people for assistance programs. For instance, to qualify for a free school lunch, a child's family income cannot exceed 130% of the Federal Poverty Line (FPL). Why? Because the people who run the programs know that the FPL is an unrealistic measure of genuine poverty. It understates the percentages of need for even basic, life-sustaining things like food for children living in poverty.

Consider this chart showing "Free And Reduced Lunch Income Qualification Levels" for the 2024-2025 school year. As a result of the additional formula we just discussed, designed to compensate for the obvious flaws in Mollie's poverty equation and the FPL, a family of four living at or below 130% of the Federal Poverty Line would qualify for subsidized (or free) lunches for their kids at school because the federal government considers these kids to be "food insecure," meaning they may not have enough food to survive on. That's why we provide those kids with a free or reduced lunch program.

Free or Reduced Lunch Income Qualification Levels July 1, 2024 - June 30, 2025		
-----	Annual Income	
Household Members	Free	Reduced
1	$19,578	$27,861
2	$26,572	$37,814
3	$33,566	$47,767
4	$40,560	$57,720
5	$47,554	$67,673
6	$54,548	$77,626
7	$61,542	$87,578
8	$68,563	$97,532
Add For Each Additional Member	+ $6,682	+ $9,509

Toward a Better Definition

As we wrap up this chapter, we need to admit that we have a problem. We've established that the FPL is not an adequate definition of poverty. But, so far, we haven't offered an alternative more adequate definition. So, what we need to talk about next is how to redefine poverty in a way that enables us to understand what poverty is, while empowering us to better serve those who experience poverty on a daily basis. To do that, we need to spend some time with the residents of Middle Classburg, America, and Povertyville, USA, people who represent two neighborhoods in a shared spiritual heritage that we refer to as the Ghetto. Now, let's go meet the family.

Reflecting and Looking Ahead

1. Reflecting on this chapter, what did you discover about America's "War on Poverty" that you didn't know before?

2. This chapter opened with a discussion of the Law Of Unintended Consequences. Describe a situation from your own experience where you saw unintended consequences that resulted from well-intended actions.

3. How did Molly Orshansky's Poverty Equation fall victim to the Law Of Unintended Consequences?

For Additional Study
For additional individual or group study, including a more in-depth look at what Scripture teaches on this topic, see the Study Guide for this book.

The Ghetto, the Garden and the Gospel

4

Trading Places

"One pretends to be rich, yet has nothing; another pretends to be poor, yet has great wealth." (Proverbs 13:7)

Thank You, Mark Twain

Do you remember your high school English literature class? If you do, maybe you remember a classic Mark Twain novel, *The Prince and the Pauper*. Set in England of 1547, the book tells the story of two young boys who are nearly identical in appearance. Tom Canty is a pauper who lives with his abusive father in a London slum neighborhood. The other boy is Prince Edward, son of King Henry VIII. Following a chance encounter, the two boys become friends and agree on a plan to trade clothes and to temporarily switch places. In their new roles, Tom works to cope with the customs and conditions of royalty, while Edward experiences the brutal life of a London pauper. Edward discovers the profound class inequality of English society and sees the harsh nature of the English judicial system, where people are burned at the stake, pilloried, flogged, branded or hanged on flimsy evidence for petty offenses. Shocked by what he discovers, Edward vows to reign with mercy and justice when he is King. Both Tom and Edward eventually return to their respective roles, better and wiser people for their experiences.

In terms of our discussion concerning poverty, both boys in this story better understood the economic status of the other. And that's what we want to do in this chapter. It's time for us to metaphorically "trade places" with our neighbors, so that we can better understand what life is like outside of Middle Classburg, America. We'll start by comparing how a transportation problem looks differently between a person living in Middle Classburg, America, a typical Middle Class community that operates with all the usual Middle Class norms, and Povertyville, USA, a typical poverty community in the United States.

The Morning the Car Wouldn't Start

It's a normal morning in Middle Classburg, America, when you head out the door to go to work. You get in your car, turn the key and nothing happens. *Okay,* you think to yourself, *I wonder what's wrong?* So, you turn the key again, and nothing happens. It's dead and you're momentarily panicked. Question: What do in Middle Classburg do when your car won't start? Answer: You call Triple A (or that roadside service your insurance company offers). They come. They check out the car. "No problem," they say, "We'll put it on the tow truck, tow it to the repair shop, and we'll give you a ride." Once there, you put down a credit/debit card for the repair because you have access to credit. Next, you call the rental car company that picks you up. Sure enough, they come, they pick you up, and you get a rental car until your car is fixed. Yes, it's been a big hassle for about three hours, but the good news is that you're on your way to work, just a little late, which your boss understands.

That's basically what happens in Middle Classburg, America. The transportation problem stayed a transportation problem temporarily until we could get it fixed. I call it the "pizza slice" life. If you have young kids (or grand-kids), you've probably gone through that stage where their food can't touch any other food on their plate, which makes it really difficult to do a trauma-free meal (I'm not a child psychologist, so don't ask!). Well, life in Middle Classburg is that same way, in that we don't like one area of our life to interfere with another. In fact, we like the parts of our life separated so much that we describe those slices as "different lives." Have you ever heard someone say, "Oh, that's my work life, and this is my home life, and that's my church life." We even use terms like "work-life balance" and "having boundaries" to describe how we separate out the different "pizza slices" of our life.

Now, let's review the same scenario, but this time, we're not residents of Middle Classburg, America. We're now living in Povertyville, USA. So, it's another typical, challenging day in Povertyville, USA, when you head out the door to go to work at your minimum-wage job(s). You get in your car, turn the key, and nothing happens. *Great*, you think to yourself. *This 15-year old piece of auto debris finally died, and at the worst possible moment.*[18] You turn the key again, and nothing happens. It's dead and you're somewhere between frustrated and panicked. Question: What do you do in Povertyville, USA? Answer: you call a family member or friend who, hopefully, knows something about cars. In Middle Classburg you call AAA, but in Povertyville you call Uncle Ray. Uncle Ray comes over, checks out your car, and says, "I don't know what's wrong with it. I can maybe fix it this weekend, but I'll give you a ride to work today." So, until Uncle Ray can fix your car, you have a transportation problem.

In Povertyville, you don't have credit that you can use to rent a car, so you have to try and find a ride to work. But finding rides to work isn't reliable, the bus takes hours, and the schedules and bus stops don't coincide with your work schedule and kids school schedules and locations. Soon, you start showing up to work late due to your transportation problem. Unfortunately, you don't have the type of job where you can show up late. As a result, your transportation problem quickly becomes something else. It becomes an employment problem, because you just lost your job(s).

And That's When Everything Else Went Wrong

What started out as a transportation problem has now become a job problem. And that deserves a quick note. Federal Minimum Wage is currently $7.25/hour. Some states and municipalities have increased the minimum wage recently. For instance, in Washington State, where I live, it's a little higher at $16.28 per hour. But according to the Living Wage Project at MIT, for a family

> What started out as a transportation problem has now become a job problem.

with one working adult (such as a single mom) and two children, the living wage needed to pay the bills and live in Washington State is $46.94/hour at a forty hour work week.[19] So, if you're a single mom in my state, you probably have two jobs. And you just lost one of your jobs. Now you aren't earning nearly enough money to pay the rent, so it isn't long before you lose your housing. What started out as a transportation problem and became a job problem has now become a housing problem. You are now effectively homeless . . . and jobless.

When you lose your housing, what do you do? Where do you go? You're forced to move in with family or friends. Let's face it, you're going to go stay with family or friends before you go to a homeless shelter. But problems soon surface. If you've ever had family over for the holidays, you probably remember how well that went. Benjamin Franklin was right when he said, "Fish and visitors begin to smell after three days," and your problem is definitely going to last longer than three days! Things don't go well, and you begin having relationship issues. All of a sudden, things get really intense and stressful. As a result, you start having health issues. You start getting sick. Where in Middle Classburg life is like pizza slices, in Povertyville life is like a ball of yarn. You pull one string and everything that is interconnected unravels rapidly.

Your transportation problem became a job problem,

which became a housing problem,

which became a relationship problem,

which has now become a healthcare problem.

We used to think that poor people had more health issues than wealthy people because they had poor access to healthcare. Then, countries like Canada and some countries in Europe began offering universal access to health care. After studying the relationship between health, wealth, and access to health care for over twenty years, Canada discovered that the wealthier you are, the healthier you are, and the poorer you are, the sicker you are. "Poverty is the No. 1 factor in determining whether Canadians live long, healthy lives, says a report from the Canadian Medical Association." [20] Why? Because our overall health isn't just about access. It's a stress issue, and ACEs demonstrated it.

A Test You Don't Want to ACE

Starting in the 1990s, people working among poverty populations began studying something they called ACEs (Adverse Childhood Experiences). The original study that would become known as ACEs was conducted by Kaiser Permanente from 1995 to 1997. Kaiser originally set out to study obesity, but as they conducted physical exams and confidential surveys about childhood experiences and current health status and behaviors they discovered a correlation between childhood abuse and neglect and household challenges and later-life health and well-being.[21] In a study of some 17,000 adults, they asked participants about such childhood experiences as abuse, neglect, a parent going to prison, and others (there were ten questions on the survey). The researchers discovered that increased levels of childhood trauma increased levels of stress and significantly increased the likelihood of having major health issues as time goes on. As someone observed, "the real gateway drug is trauma."

For example, researchers found that people with an ACE score of 4 are twice as likely to be smokers and seven times more likely to be alcoholic. Having an ACE score of 4 increases the risk of emphysema or chronic bronchitis by nearly 400 percent and attempted suicide by 1200 percent. People with high ACE scores are more likely to be violent, to have more marriages, more broken bones, more drug prescriptions, more mental health issues, and more autoimmune diseases. People with an ACE score of 6 or higher are at risk of their life span being shortened by twenty years.[22]

Figure 2. Mechanisms by which Adverse Childhood Experiences (ACEs) Lead to Poor Outcomes in Adulthood

Death

Early death

Disease, disability, and social problems

Adoption of health-risk behaviors

Social, emotional, and cognitive impairment

Disrupted neurodevelopment

Adverse childhood experiences

Conception

Source: Centers for Disease Control and Prevention

The reason for these health impacts is simple: stress. Welcome to the ongoing tension and stress of living in Povertyville, USA, the condition many of our friends, families and neighbors live in every day. They worry about some domino in their life falling (such as transportation), which leads to more dominoes falling (jobs, housing, broken relationships, homelessness, etc.). In order to cope, they might turn to substance abuse or crime (and one almost always leads to the other).

In Povertyville, USA, life doesn't consist of cleanly separated pizza slices like in Middle Classburg. Rather, life in Povertyville consists of an interconnected ball of yarn, where one thing intersects with every other thing, and where we lack the resources to maintain a stable living environment. The realities of life in Povertyville demand that we find a new and better definition of poverty. And that's where we want to go next.

Reflecting and Looking Ahead

1. Reflecting on this chapter, what did you learn about the differences between those living in Middle Classburg, America, and those living in Povertyville, USA?

2. What did you discover about your own economic status? Which of the two communities did you find yourself identifying with the most?

3. We opened this chapter with Mark Twain's story, *The Prince And The Pauper*. Which do you think would be easier: for a pauper to live as a prince, or for a prince to live as a pauper? Why? Likewise, which do you think would be easier: for a resident of Middle Classburg to live in Povertyville or for a resident of Povertyville to live in Middle Classburg? Why?

For Additional Study

For additional individual or group study, including a more in-depth look at what Scripture teaches on this topic, see the Study Guide for this book.

5

The Time Is Now

"For everything there is a season, and a time for every matter under heaven." (Ecclesiastes 3:1)

Defining Poverty

In this chapter, we will be doing two things. First, we will be offering a more realistic definition of poverty. Second, we will explore the concept of how time functions differently in cultures of poverty. By way of review up to this point, we've discussed the three types of poverty, President Johnson's War on Poverty, and Mollie Orshansky's monetary definition of poverty. In the process, we concluded that the official government definition of poverty (Mollie's poverty equation, which produced the Federal Poverty Level) is not a realistic definition. It simply leaves out too many factors which contribute to poverty. What we haven't done yet is offer an alternative and more realistic definition of poverty. Therefore, here is the definition of poverty that we will use to guide our discussion moving forward:

"Poverty is that point at which you lack the daily resources needed to maintain a stable environment."

Notice this new definition of poverty isn't a monetary definition? It isn't about earning money. It's about having stable resources. The reason is that poverty is a result of a lack of many resources, such as food, affordable housing, mental health, education, proper identification, living wage employment, and more. In fact, I would argue that there are eighteen physical and mental resources you need to have in place to be out of poverty and to maintain a stable environment in the United States. Along with these eighteen physical and mental resources, there are also relational and spiritual resources which work to either stabilize or destabilize the other resources. In fact, any time just one area is the focus of our attention, the other areas come screaming to the forefront as glaring holes.

Let me give an example. When I first started

in ministry, I had this idea that, as people in need came into our church, we would help them with food and then financial counseling. So, I studied all of the best budgeting tools by Dave Ramsey and Crown Financial. When I sat down with my first client I was confident as I told the person in need,

"We are going to do a budget."

The man in need then took $10 out of his pocket, set it on the table, and said,

"Ok, that's all I have. I don't know when I will get more. How do you want to budget that?"

Suddenly, the realization came crashing down on me that all of the best and expensive financial budgeting tools require a stable income. Otherwise, they don't work. So, those got thrown out the window! After thinking for a minute I said,

"Ok, let's look at jobs."

"Ok," said the man, *"I would love a job, but I don't have an ID or mailing address and it costs $50 for me to get an ID."*

"OK, let me see what we can do to pay for your ID," I said.

"That would be great," said the client, *"I also have a criminal record and have child support fines in another state. This state will not give me a drivers license until I pay those fines in the other state."*

Just like that, the realization came to me that stability requires resources and a lot of them, beyond just money.

Many people come to the problems of poverty and homelessness with ill conceived and simplistic solutions. Each of these fails to take into account the complexity of resources it takes to successfully navigate our lives. As such, most solutions offered for these problems come dreadfully short and often devolve into simply throwing money at solutions that have little to no hope at solving the actual problems associated with a scarcity of resources. Understanding the profound impact of resource scarcity and prolonged toxic stress on individuals in poverty is critical. This chronic stress can fundamentally alter brain function and shape worldviews in ways that those in more stable circumstances might find hard to comprehend. Consider the concept of time—a straightforward and universally understood dimension for many. Yet, in communities deeply affected by poverty, such as our hypothetical "Povertyville, USA," perceptions of time can significantly diverge from those held in "Middle Classburg." This difference often leads to misunderstandings and frustrations among mission teams and employers working with individuals from backgrounds of generational poverty. Here's why this happens. Let me explain.

A Biblical Understanding of Time

You might not know the 60s rock group, *The Byrds*. But the chances are good that you remember their international hit song, "Turn! Turn! Turn! (To Everything There Is a Season)," which hit the music charts at #80 on October 23, 1965, and went on to hit #1 on the Billboard Hot 100 chart on December 4, 1965. Written by Pete Seeger in the late 1950s, the song is interesting for two reasons. First, it's interesting because it is essentially a word-for-word adaptation of a passage from the Old Testament book of Ecclesiastes (3:1-8). But it's interesting for a second reason. It expresses what we could describe as a Middle Classburg understanding of time: a time for everything, and everything in its time.

Now, at this point you may be scratching your head and wondering what understanding *time* has to do with understanding poverty. The connection is this: *living in poverty changes a person's view of time.* For those living in Povertyville, USA, linear time doesn't work the same. Instead, life becomes a *season* or *seasons*. And that deserves an explanation. So, let's do a brief biblical word study on *time*.

> Living in poverty changes a person's view of time.

The New Testament has three primary words for time, besides common words like day or night. The first word for time is *chronos*, what we would call linear time. It's normal time measured by length or duration, measured from Point A to Point B. Most of us arrange our daily and weekly activities according to a *chronos* understanding of time. The second word for time is *aionios*, meaning eternal, never-ending, or everlasting. It appears forty-two times in Scripture, specifically in the phrase eternal life, describing what every believer in Jesus looks forward to: unending life in the Kingdom of God. The third word for time is *kairos*. While often translated as time, *kairos* can also convey the sense of a season -- time measured differently, not by its length or duration, but by its character, its significance, or its focus. For example, measured by *chronos*, the ministry of Jesus lasted roughly three-and-a-half years. But Luke also describes that three-and-a-half year period as a season (*kairos*) of divine visitation (Luke 19:44).

Planning the Future vs. the Season of Now

This may be a difficult concept to comprehend, but how we view time often differs if we come from a Middle Class mindset versus a Poverty mindset. In the United States, particularly in middle-class communities, there's a tendency to follow a linear perception of time, organizing life in a sequential order. We meticulously plan our days, weeks, and even years, thanks to tools like Google Calendar, aligning with the chronological (*chronos*) concept of time. This methodical approach allows for a structured prioritization of tasks and activities well into the future, epitomizing the saying, "A time for every purpose under heaven."

Contrastingly, for those residing in impoverished circumstances, time adopts a non-linear, immediate seasonal (*kairos*) nature. In these environments, the pressing needs of the moment dictate actions, making the present the focal point of life. This *season of now* mentality stems from the constant battle with instability and crisis management, eliminating the luxury of long-term planning. Immediate concerns like securing daily meals, shelter for the night, and day-to-day survival take precedence, overshadowing any future aspirations.

Moreover, the experience of poverty profoundly alters one's temporal perspective. While middle-class individuals might be oriented towards future planning and achievement, scheduling their lives around calendars and planners, those in poverty prioritize the urgent needs of today. This difference in time perception can lead to misunderstandings and adjustments, especially in contexts where cultural interpretations of time vary significantly, such as in Guatemala or parts of Africa, where time is more flexible and event-driven.

Depending on how prevalent poverty is in the culture, our understanding of time becomes less rigid and less linear, and it becomes more loose and flexible.

It even gets, well, unusual and is often frustrating for those with more of a Middle Class mindset. For example, in Guatemala (where 75% of the population lives below the national poverty line and 58% of the population meets the income requirement for extreme poverty), a morning meeting may be delayed two hours and start in the afternoon, and my afternoon meeting might not happen today and will be pushed to tomorrow.

African time, however, tends to be even more flexible and seasons of time happen daily. What I mean by this is in a lot of Africa time is not chronological and fixed. Rather, it works this way. I'm doing whatever I'm doing now, and when I'm done with that I'll do what I'm doing next. As a result, we see refugees come to the United States, get a job, and show up forty-five minutes late for work. When their boss asks, "Where were you?" they'll say, "I was talking to my cousin." That's a perfectly valid explanation for an African in their culture. Does that work for an American employer? No. So, yes, there are definite cultural differences when it comes to time.[23]

The Impact of How We Understand Time

This non-linear view of time is incredibly impactful in several ways. One of the ways is how our view of time influences crime. This connection was first observed by a man named Reuven Feuerstein, a Holocaust survivor and sociologist. Studying poor Jewish youth after World War II, Feuerstein noticed that kids coming out of the Holocaust were committing a lot of crimes. He wanted to know why that was happening. From his studies, Feuerstein created a paradigm to explain what he was seeing. According to Feuerstein, living in an unpredictable environment (such as chronic poverty), where you're just focused on today, affects how you respond to situations.[24]

Feuerstein's observations evolved into this thought progression, kids living in unpredictable environments may not develop the ability to plan:

1. If you can't plan, you can't predict
2. If you can't predict, you can't identify cause-and-effect
3. If you can't identify cause-and-effect, you can't identify consequences
4. If you can't identify consequences, you'll have difficulty controlling impulsivity

5. If you can't control impulsivity, you'll have an inclination towards criminal behavior.

This is why in public schools teachers will talk about a kid just walking down the hallway who suddenly reaches out and punches another kid. When the teacher asks, "Why did you do that? Now you're gonna be expelled from school," the kid answers, "Well, he looked at me wrong. What do you mean I'm gonna be expelled from school?" When the teacher says, "Well, yeah, you can't be hitting other kids at school," the kid responds, "Well, I didn't know I'd be expelled for doing that." There is a disconnect from the immediate action and the consequence of that action.

Kids immersed in poverty have more difficulty defining or understanding cause-and-effect relationships. This is an important concept, especially in education, because standardized achievement tests tend to focus on your ability to identify cause-and-effect relationships! Even the math portion of many standardized tests currently being used in public schools have been changed to word problems which require students to identify cause-and-effect relationships. Is it any surprise that our poor kids score worse across the board on state-mandated standardized tests, even when they are in the same classroom with Middle Class students?

Two Practical Tools

If you're working or engaging with individuals in poverty and trying to help them with impulsivity issues, I want to offer a couple of practical tools that you can use. The first tool is daily written goals. If you're mentoring a kid at school, or someone at your workplace, have them write out their goal for today. Not tomorrow. Not next week. Not next year. Just today. Have a written daily goal. At the end of the day you can come back to it and ask, "Did we get it accomplish it or not?"

If you think this is a small or insignificant thing, you are wrong. In what has become a legendary commencement address at the University of Texas, Austin, in 2014, Admiral William H. McRaven, Commander of United States Special Operations Command, gave the graduating class the same basic advice I'm offering here.

"If you want to change the world, start off by making your bed. If you make your bed every morning you will have accomplished the first task of the day. It will give you a small sense of pride, and it will encourage you to do another task, and another, and another, and by the end of the day that one task completed will have turned into many tasks completed." [25]

Admiral McRaven's point mirrors our own. Small accomplishments, like daily goals, can eventually lead to greater accomplishments. Let me offer a real-world example of this principle. At the homeless shelter I run, we implemented written daily goals (what we call a Daily SMART Goal). As a result, we saw the average length of stay in the shelter decrease by 15 days. At $42 per person per day average shelter cost and with 100 people per day in our emergency family shelter that 15 days amounts to a $63,000 savings, simply by writing daily goals. Setting daily goals is simple, practical and effective!

The second practical tool is to teach backwards. If you're training an employee, mentoring a student, or discipling someone from a poverty background who operates with a skewed view of time, one of the things you can do is to teach backwards from a goal to a specific task to be accomplished. Now, for most of us this is unusual because it tends to be the opposite of Middle Class thinking or planning. In the Middle Class, we tend to think in terms of steps forward. We're going to take this step, and then we'll take the next step. With the proper number of steps forward, we'll reach our goal. But, when you're working with somebody in poverty, sometimes it's more helpful to start with the goal you want to reach and work backwards. For example, let's say you're helping them plan a trip. It might go like this in three steps:

Step 1

You: "What do you need to do before you leave on your trip?"

Them: "I need to get to the airport."

Step 2

You: "Okay, great. How are you going to get to the airport? What are you gonna do before that?"

Them: "I need to get a ride."

Step 3

You: "Good, you need to get a ride. What do you need to do before that?"

Them: "I need to actually book the airfare."

As you can see, we're working backwards. In the end, you accomplish the same thing, but you help them work backwards from the desired goal (the trip) to the tasks along the way. This is often a more helpful way for a lot of folks in generational poverty to work, particularly kids. You can even draw this out, or have them draw little things out on a notepad or a piece of paper. It helps them work on these impulsivity

> For some families living in poverty, planning for two weeks out is like you or me scheduling an appointment a year from now!

tests. Eventually, we get from one day to two days. We make a goal for tomorrow, then we make a goal for the week, and then we make a goal for two weeks. For some families living in poverty, planning for two weeks out is like you or me scheduling an appointment a year from now! They're thinking, I have no idea where I'm going to be two weeks from now. I don't know where I'm gonna be staying, what we're gonna be eating, or even if I'm gonna be in this city two weeks from now. Remember, in the unstable environment of poverty, things change fast.

This is the challenge of trying to tell time (and to plan) during a season of poverty in Povertyville, USA. But a different understanding of time is not the only characteristic which sets the residents of Povertyville apart from their cousins in Middle Classburg. There are six distinguishing characteristics. In the next chapter, we'll take a look at the other five: Time, Money, Worldview, Emphasis, Driving Force, Mental Model.

Reflecting and Looking Ahead

1. Reflecting on this chapter, what did you learn about the different ways people understand time? Discuss a personal example you have witnessed of how people around you treat time differently.

2. Think of examples of people you are working with (in a professional environment, or in a discipleship situation) where the two practical tools discussed in this chapter (daily written goals and teaching backwards) might be helpful. Describe one of those situations.

3. In this chapter, we defined poverty as follows: Poverty is the point at which one lacks the daily resources needed for a stable environment. Do you agree or disagree? Explain.

For Additional Study

For additional individual or group study, including a more in-depth look at what Scripture teaches on this topic, see the Study Guide for this book.

The Ghetto, the Garden and the Gospel

6

Understanding Our Differences

"Here this, all peoples! Give ear, all inhabitants of the world,
Both low and high, Rich and poor together!
My mouth shall speak wisdom;
The meditation of my heart shall be understanding."
(Psalm 49: 1-3)

Earlier, in chapter 4, we tried to imagine what it would be like to trade places with those living in poverty. Next, in chapter 5, we looked at how two people, a resident of Middle Classburg and someone living in Povertyville, each understand time. We discovered some profound differences between these two mindsets. For a person with a Middle Class mindset, time tends to be future-focused. We have goals and plans for the future. We take classes to better understand issues and how to plan for that future. But for someone living in poverty, their mindset is different. Their time-focus is on the present. Right now. I'm worried about today, and nothing else. For those living in the season of poverty, the time is always now.

But how we understand time is not the only difference between these two economic neighbors. In fact, there are six key characteristics or differences which distinguish the residents of Middle Classburg, America, from the residents of Povertyville, USA. I want to use the chart on the next page to identify those characteristics, and highlight how the residents of Middle Classburg, America, and Povertyville, USA, tend to see and experience life differently. It's time to better understand our differences.[26]

Money: Manage Versus Spend

The first major characteristic we looked at in the previous chapter involved our view of time. The second characteristic involves how we view *Money*. In the mindset of Middle Classburg, America, we tend to regard money as something to be managed. Money isn't just something we use to pay the bills. It's also something we use to plan for the future. We use online banking tools and programs like Quicken to manage our money. We have a bank account, a savings account, and even an investment account. At our job, we may have a

401(k) retirement account to help us save for a future retirement. We may even have a budget. In other words, in a Middle Class worldview, we practice some type of money management with a view toward planning for the future.

Understanding Our Differences		
Characteristic	Middle Class	Poverty
Time	Future	Present/Now
Money		
Worldview		
Emphasis		
Driving Force		
Mental Model		
Definition		

In the mindset of Povertyville, USA, things are a little different. The tendency is not to manage money, but to spend it when you get it. Why? Because you don't know when (or if) you're ever going to get some again. And, in the time-focus of now, there are things you need today. Also, you don't always have a safe place to keep money. This is something that people outside of Povertyville often get very upset about.

For example, when Hurricane Katrina devastated New Orleans in August of 2005, we saw images of people being placed in FEMA trailers for temporary housing. In addition, FEMA tried to speed up some payments to Katrina survivors by handing out $2,000 debit cards, meant to cover basics of food, clothing, and deposits on apartments. However, as many news stations reported, and the Government Accountability Office (GAO) later confirmed, some people had used that money for frivolous things like getting hair and nails done, buying big screen TVs, or, as an official GAO report dryly noted, some money was "used for adult entertainment, bail bond services and weapons purchase, which don't appear to be items or services that are essential to satisfy disaster related essential needs."[27] Additionally, $24.3 million dollars (62.8%) of the debit card money was withdrawn in the form of cash from ATMs instead of being used via the cards. The need for cash would make sense if these funds were distributed in areas without power; however, most of these debit cards were issued at evacuation locations in cities not impacted by the storm, like at the Houston Astrodome. When asked why they spent the FEMA funds on such things, rather than finding an apartment, many people responded by saying things like, "I had never seen $2,000 before, and I didn't know if I would ever see that kind of money again. My kids were driving me nuts because they had nothing to do, so, I bought the big screen TV."

Let's take a moment and expand on the importance of TVs in poverty. When you visit the home of someone living in poverty, it's very common to walk in the door and see a couch or maybe a mattress on the floor. Then, when you turn around, you'll often see a ginormous big-screen TV. Maybe the biggest one you've ever seen in your life. Why? Think about it for just a moment. In Middle Classburg, you and I have money for vacations and vacation time off from work. If our boss is difficult or if work is stressful, we'll take a sick day or we'll go on vacation and get away from things for a little while. However, people living in poverty often don't have those work benefits or those costly options. Instead, that oversized big-screen TV becomes the poor man's alternative to a vacation. The house is filled with people, it's loud, and he can escape the chaos by just focusing on TV. There's more. Besides TV, you'll often hear loud music. Let's just turn up the music and zone out. Better yet, let's invite even more people over and have a party and escape for a while.

When I lived in Denton, Texas, we lived in a neighborhood where a fiesta happened nearly every night. At night, we could hear loud Tejano music playing and people laughing and cheering. [28] Why? Because the relationships are what's important in that environment. So, why not invite people over, have a party, turn the music up, and leave your problems behind for a little while?

Worldview: Regional Versus Ultra-Local

The third difference between the residents of Middle Classburg, America, and the residents of Povertyville, USA, has to do with our perspective, or what philosophers call our *Worldview*.[29] Borrowed from German philosophy, our worldview is our world in a mental box. It's the mental framework we use to see, understand, and make sense of our world on a daily basis. The worldview of Middle Classburg tends to be

> Our Worldview is our world in a mental box.

regional. We watch the news to learn what's happening in our area. We'll watch some news on a state and national level, along with a tiny bit of international news. Unless we have some personal tie to the place being featured, we're good with the ten-second news bite on some major international issue, and then we want to get back to our local news and weather. So, our focus in Middle Classburg tends to be regional -- what's happening in our area, our city and our county.

In Povertyville, USA, however, the worldview tends to be local -- very local, even ultra-local. Not just my city, but my neighborhood, even from this street to that street. Not only is my worldview ultra-local, but so is my identity. This is my neighborhood. This is where my family and I feel safe. This is where we know our neighbors. So, I'm going to protect this neighborhood. This ultra-local identity

> In Povertyville, USA . . . the worldview tends to be local, very local -- even ultra-local.

sometimes produces social problems, such as gangs. Gangs typically have a strong ultra-local identity and they will protect their turf.

This ultra-local focus creates other interesting results. For example, you might get involved in a Big Brothers Big Sisters program. You decide to take the child you mentor out for ice cream on the other side of the highway and you discover that they've never been to that side of the highway before! They're twelve-years-old and they have grown up in that city their whole life, but they've never been to the other side of that highway, just a couple of blocks from where they have spent their whole life.. But that's what happens when your worldview in Povertyville produces an ultra-local identity and you have limited transportation.

Emphasis: Quality Versus Quantity

The fourth difference between Middle Classburg and Povertyville has to do with our *Emphasis*: quality versus quantity. To illustrate this, let's contrast a meal in Middle Classburg, America, with a meal in Povertyville. In Middle Classburg, America, when you and I go out to eat, something interesting happens.

> In Middle Classburg, America, the emphasis is on the quality.

Your waiter or waitress serves your food and disappears for a few minutes while you begin eating. Shortly after that they come back and ask you a question. It happens every single time. What's the question? "How's everything tasting?" Why do they do that? They do it because quality is important. In Middle Classburg, America, the emphasis is on the quality.

Now, let's go out to eat, again. Only this time, you're eating in the home of one of your cousins in Povertyville, USA, who lives in generational poverty. This home could actually be in any poverty community in the world and the same thing will happen. They are going to feed you. Even if it's the last food that they have, they will feed the guests. As you're

> In Povertyville, USA, quantity is more important than quality.

eating and you're just about finished, your host will ask you this question. "Did you have enough?" Notice how this is a very different question than the one our waiter or waitress asked us back in the restaurant. You respond graciously, "Yes, thank you. I'm stuffed," at which point they likely will put more food on your plate. Why? Because in Povertyville, quantity is more important than quality.

Let me illustrate this with a story. Several years ago, my wife and I had a twelve year old boy over to our house for a Bar-B-Que. His parents had died in an earthquake in Haiti. He was adopted by a woman in Spokane, Washington, but she contracted cancer and passed away. Now, he was being raised by his adopted grandmother who lives on a very limited income and she was unable to care for him. So another family, who are friends of ours, expressed interest in adopting him. They brought him over to our house for a Bar-B-Que so we could meet him.

Soon, this kid is eating everything in sight! Non-stop eating, eating, eating, eating, eating . . . just non-stop. The mother who was interested in adopting him asks him a question, "What's your favorite food?" The boy says, "My favorite? I don't know, but I like steak, and I like chicken, and I like corn, and I like mashed potatoes, and I like green beans, and I like pizza, and I like eggs, and I like bacon, and I like sausage, and I like oranges, and I like grapefruit . . ."

For the next few minutes this boy went on and on, naming every food he could think of. By this point we're all giggling because he obviously did not understand the question. So, the mother interrupts him with another question, "Ok, ok, maybe this will be easier. What do you not like?" His answer brought reality to our barbecue, "I don't like it when we don't have food." His answer produced instant tears in the eyes of the barbecue-goers. Here is a kid, living in our community, who obviously has been hungry and going without food. That's why there's a difference in emphasis between quantity versus quality in Povertyville, USA. Scarcity.

These are the types of things that you see in Generational Poverty, and they're happening in your community and in every community all over our country and in every country around the world. Where resources are scarce, there will be an emphasis on quantity-over-quality. It's also why you'll hear some strange compliments in other cultures where poverty and food insecurity are prevalent.

> Where resources are scarce, there will be an emphasis on quantity over quality.

For example, in Latin American cultures, it's not uncommon to call somebody "gordo" (Spanish for "fat") as a term of endearment. Could you imagine calling your child or a coworker, "Hey, Fat Guy"? No. But in Latin American cultures of poverty, it's often a term of endearment and you will hear it regularly.

Additionally, in some African cultures, you might hear someone try and compliment another person by saying, "Wow, you're looking really fat today!" As you can imagine, this is not the favorite complement for our American missionaries, particularly our female missionaries. However, in that culture, it's meant as a compliment because, in a place where people have starved to death historically, if you have enough food to look overweight, then you must be doing well financially.

This emphasis on quantity-over-quality in cultures of poverty creates some interesting problems here in America. If you live in a poor neighborhood like

Understanding Our Differences

Povertyville, USA, where do you buy food and you don't have transportation? Probably at a local convenience store. And what kind of food do you get at those places? Junk food, or unhealthy, highly-processed, very sugary junk food.

As a result, for the first time in human history we're experiencing an epidemic of obesity coupled with poverty in America. We're seeing children in poverty with high rates of both obesity and diabetes, due to access to cheap junk food and a corresponding lack of access to affordable

> It's estimated that 23.5 million Americans live in an area without a grocery store or healthy food options.

healthy food. Or they lack the ability to properly store, make, or cook healthy food. This issue of food availability in poor neighborhoods has led to the identification of a phenomenon known as urban food deserts. These are low-income or impoverished areas, usually in urban environments, with limited-access to healthy food. This means it's an area where the residents are more than one mile away from a large grocery store or supermarket, where residents without reliable transportation don't have access to healthy food options. It's estimated that 23.5 million Americans live in an area without a grocery store or healthy food options.[30]

While food is an obvious area where you can see this emphasis on quantity over quality in poverty, it is not the only area. In fact, it is also very common to see hoarding of things or an inability to throw something away, particularly among seniors.

Driving Force: Achievement Versus Relationships

The fifth difference between Middle Classburg and Povertyville has to do with the *Driving Force*, which is another way of saying the reason or motivation to keep going.

In Middle Classburg, America, personal achievement drives the engine of ambition. From self-help books to diet programs and fads, the middle class is perpetually seeking ways to enhance individual success. Pursuits such as acquiring degrees, certifications, and gym memberships reflect the relentless quest for self-improvement. This ethos prioritizes efficiency, often manifesting in the quantification of accomplishments, such as the number of books read or pounds lost. However, the emphasis on achievement can sometimes overshadow genuine empathy in endeavors like church outreach programs, where the focus shifts towards serving a large number of people rather than fostering meaningful relationships and life transformation.

Conversely, in Povertyville, USA, relationships reign supreme as the cornerstone of survival. In this milieu, the reliance on close-knit bonds for everyday necessities like childcare, car repairs, and transportation underscores the vital role of interpersonal connections. Here, empathy is prized, as it forms the bedrock of communal support networks. Yet, the absence of broader resources often limits opportunities for upward mobility, resulting in a culture where survival takes precedence over individual advancement. This distinction highlights the critical need for empathy-driven initiatives in combating poverty, where genuine relationships serve as catalysts for sustainable change. Effective ministry is a ministry that is living out the great commission, as defined by Jesus in Matthew 28: 18-20, by producing disciples. We will examine this in detail later in the book

Mental Model: Pizza Slice Versus Ball of Yarn

Our sixth (but by no means final!) difference involves our *Mental Model*. A mental model is an internal visual of an external reality. It's the metaphoric picture we form in our head to try and help explain what something is like. As we mentioned earlier in chapter 4, the mindset among the residents of Middle Classburg is segmented like slices of pizza, and we don't like the pieces touching each other. But, in Povertyville, USA, life is all interconnected, like a ball of yarn. What happens when you try to pull one string in a ball of yarn? It all comes with it. No separation! This is why, when you're talking to somebody in generational poverty and they're telling you a story, that story often doesn't go straight to the point. Instead, they will wind around to other details and other things, and leave you wondering, "Where are you going with all this?" Why? Because, from their perspective, their life is a winding road, one big ball of yarn, and everything's connected to everyone and everything else. Despite middle class confusion about this, to them, it makes perfect sense.

Understanding Our Differences

Two Definitions

As we conclude this chapter, lets do two things. *First,* let's define what we mean by Middle Class. Earlier, in chapter 5, we defined poverty as follows:

Poverty is the point at which you lack the daily resources needed to maintain a stable environment.

Now it's time for us to define what we mean by Middle Class. Here it is:

Middle Class is that point at which you have sufficient resources for a stable environment today, and enough resources to plan for tomorrow.

Secondly, there is a temptation to view the chart on the following page and allow it to confirm our preconceived notions. Some people close the book at this point and think they have got it, that they know. However, great caution should be applied here because the roots of poverty and what the Bible instructs Christians to do about it require believers to keep reading. By this book's end, your perspective on these charted items and your role in them will shift significantly. So look over this chart for reference to understand where we have been, but then continue the journey with us to find out where we are going.

Now that we've defined both poverty and Middle Class, and have explored some of our differences, it's time to get to know a real family of the residents of Povertyville, USA.

Reflecting and Looking Ahead

1. Reflecting on this chapter, what one new thing did you learn about the differences between those living in Middle Classburg, America, and those living in Povertyville, USA? Why did that one thing stand out to you? Explain. How has this chapter helped you better understand people living in generational poverty?

2. How narrow or broad is your worldview: Local? Regional? National? Global? How much do you know about people living in poverty outside of your immediate community?

3. How did this chapter force you to examine your own attitudes toward money? Are you a spender or a saver? What do your money habits say about your own social/economic mindset?

For Additional Study

For additional individual or group study, including a more in-depth look at what Scripture teaches on this topic, see the Study Guide for this book.

Understanding Our Differences		
Characteristic	Middle Class	Poverty
Time	Future	Present/Now
Money	Manage/Save/Invest	Spend
Worldview	City/Region/State	Ultra Local
Emphasis	Quality	Quantity
Driving Force	Achievement	Relationships
Mental Model	A Segmented Pizza	A Ball of Yarn
Definition	*Middle Class is that point at which you have sufficient resources for a stable environment today, and enough resources to plan for tomorrow.*	*Poverty is that point at which you lack the daily resources needed to maintain a stable environment.*

7

Looking Closer at a Family in Poverty

"Those who were not my people I will call 'my people
And her who was not beloved I will call 'beloved'."
(Romans 9:25)

A Family in Generational Poverty

In this chapter, we will focus our attention on one particular family caught up in the vortex of generational poverty. Our story begins when Sara was ten-years-old. The graphic below shows Sara's family tree.

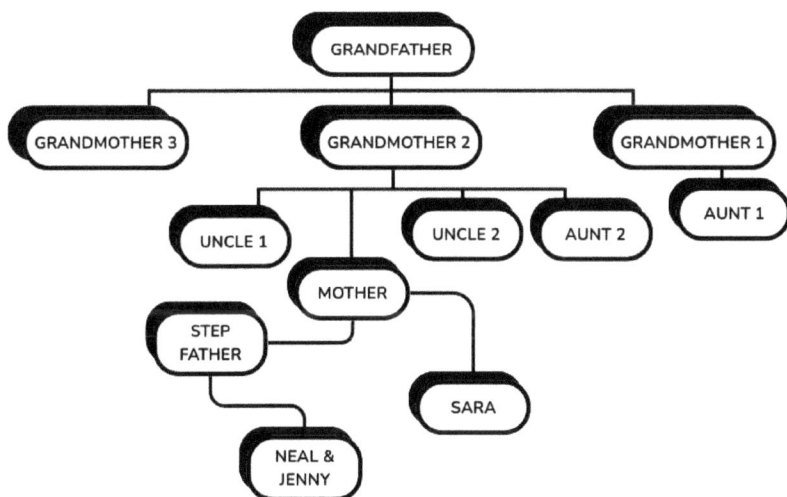

One of the first things we noticed about Sara's family tree is that Sara has three grandmothers. Yes, Grandpa gets around. It's very common for men in generational poverty to be characterized as either lovers or fighters. Note that I am making a generalization here which may not always be the case. But it is common that men in cultures of generational poverty tend to be either lovers or fighters. Lovers tend to have multiple sexual partners. They are with a woman for a while and then the opportunity arises to be with another woman, and if they have difficulty controlling impulsivity (as we've already discussed), then they might take advantage of that opportunity. Does Grandma #1 like that very much? No, she doesn't. Do the kids like that very much? No, they don't. This behavior doesn't go over very well in the home. As a result, dad ends up leaving, mom kicks dad out, or the kids say, "We don't need you, so you can go." In generational poverty, this is a common pattern for men who are lovers.

Men who are fighters on the other hand, often use violence to settle disputes So they often end up either in jail or dead. There is, however, actually one healthy place to end up for men who are fighters in America - the military. Military service can be attractive for young men raised in generational poverty. You will often find military recruiting offices in poverty communities. Lastly, men, particularly in immigrant communities, will migrate for work. All three of these instances cause men to not be in the home.[31]

Matriarchal Households

The fact that men are not often present, households in poverty communities are often built around a matriarchal structure.

In Sara's family tree, Grandpa has moved on to Grandmother #3, so Grandmother #2 is running the household for Sara's line of the family. This is so common that a complete culture can develop around the strong grandmother/caregiver role. This also impacts the church in the United States in several ways when doing urban missions. For example, if you're working in an African-American community, one of the first things you need to do is to identify the grandma who runs the show for that neighborhood. There usually is one, and while she may admit that she isn't everybody's grandma, everyone in that neighborhood treats her like their grandma. They look up to her, ask her advice, and seek her out when they need help. In biblical terms, this grandma becomes the "person of peace" -- a person of influence who can help you reach the entire neighborhood.[32]

Irresponsible Kids

Let's go back to Sara's family tree.

Sara doesn't know her dad, but she lives with her mom and her step-dad. She also has a half-brother, Neil, and a sister, Jenny. Mom and step-dad are both addicts, so mom prostitutes herself to support her addiction. Question: Who's taking care of Neil and Jenny? Answer: Sara. That's right. Sara, who is ten years old, is taking care of her half-brother Neil, who is six years old, and her toddler sister, Jenny. In communities of generational poverty, kids taking care of kids is very common. Sometimes, because of all of the stress and pressures these kids are under, they get labeled as slow or irresponsible because they tend to have more difficulty keeping up in school.

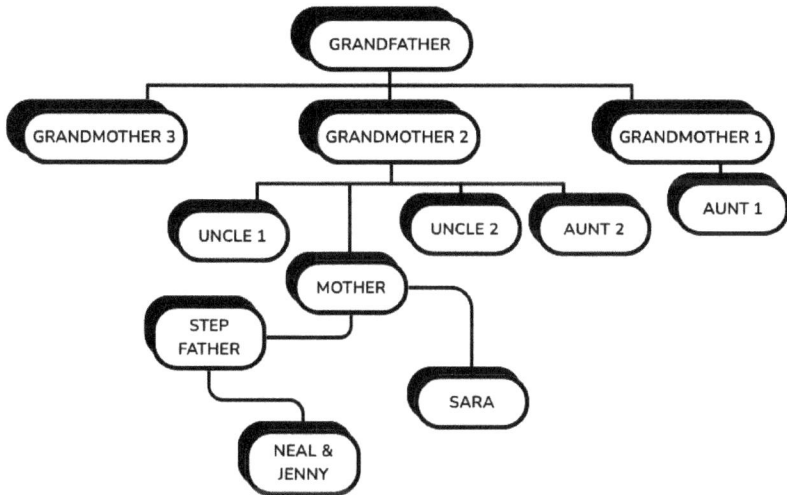

Let me give you an example of what we're talking about. When I lived in Denton, Texas, there was a middle school boy who kept getting detention because he kept arriving late for his first-period class. This kid kept showing up late, getting tardies, the tardies would add up to getting detentions, and his teacher labeled him "irresponsible." But when someone took him aside and had a conversation with him here's what they discovered. He is fourteen years old, and his mom works the night shift and the graveyard shift back-to-back. So, he is responsible for making dinner for his brother and sister, making sure they do their homework, giving them baths, and putting them to bed. In the morning, he gets them up, dresses them, feeds them breakfast, and walks them almost two miles to their school. He then turns around and runs almost two miles back the other direction to his middle school, where he shows up late.[33]

Now, is that an irresponsible kid? No! He's probably the most responsible fourteen-year-old you've ever met. But he was getting labeled "irresponsible" because he was showing up late for school and no one took the time to find out why. He eventually would start showing up on time. Do you want to know how they solved the problem? They bought him a $5 alarm clock and the Principal at his brother and sister's elementary school allowed them to enter the school a few minutes early each day so their brother could make it to school on time after dropping them

> Problem Solving 101 in Povertyville, USA starts with building relationships with those living in poverty in order to discover how best to help.

off. Here is a child who was given detentions for half a year and labeled "irresponsible" over a problem that could have been solved with a $5 alarm clock and a conversation. That's what happens when we assume and don't take the time to actually ask questions and try to understand the situation that our neighbors are in. Problem Solving 101 in Povertyville, USA starts with building relationships with those living in poverty in order to discover how best to help.

Back to our family tree. So, mom and step-dad are addicts, which does not lend itself to keeping stable jobs. If you can't keep a stable job, then you don't have money. If you don't have money, you can't pay the rent. So, where do they go when they can't pay the rent? Grandma's house! And they aren't alone. In this real-life example, Grandma, Uncle 1, Uncle 2, Aunt 1, Mom, Step-Dad, Sara, Neil, and Jenny are all living together in a 458-square-foot efficiency house. That's nine people living in 458 square feet, and all of the adults have addiction issues (either substance or alcohol). As a result, the kids are raising the kids. Additionally, Child Protective Services (CPS) will quickly tell you that when you have a lot of people living in a household, you will see a spike of incidents involving physical and sexual abuse. Sara, Neal and Jenny all suffered from physical and sexual abuse. This is something that's not widely discussed. However, in the United States, across all socio-economic categories, not just in poverty, statistics tell us that one-in-four women/girls will be physically or sexually abused by the time they're eighteen years old. For boys, the number is one in six. However, in Povertyville, USA, all of those numbers increase to greater than one in four and greater than one in six. A lot of our kids living in generational poverty are dealing with these types of extreme, life-altering traumas in their homes. Children who are unable to escape those environments often suppress the trauma which can lead to attachment, relationship, and substance abuse issues in adulthood.

"I'm Staying on the Couch"

Eventually mom and step-dad get arrested and hauled off to jail. CPS comes in, looks at all the adults living in this tiny 458 square-foot efficiency house, and says, "No, this isn't a fit environment for these kids." So where does CPS put Sara? It turns out that Sara has a living relative, her grandfather, who's now living with grandmother #3. So, Sara moves in with Grandpa and Grandma #3. Where did Neal and Jenny go? They're sent off to live with their dad's side of the family.

Now, Sara thinks that it's her job to raise her little brother and sister, but now they've been pulled apart. Sara, who is used to caring for herself and her little brother and sister, is now being parented by a non-blood relative, Grandma #3, and her grandfather. Does that situation go very well? No. There's a lot of tension, arguing, and resentment. Sara decides to go and live with her aunt, who's underneath Grandma #1. That situation lasts for a little while, but she eventually ends up moving back and forth and back and forth between her aunt and grandfather and Grandma #3.

In cultures of poverty, you tend to see this type of constant movement, back and forth, so much that a person in poverty often won't tell you where they live, rather they'll tell you where they stay, and they'll ask you, "Where do you stay?" Why? Because, for the residents of Povertyville, USA, where they live is not a constant -- it's a moving target. So they'll say, "I'm staying with my aunt," or, "I'm staying with my friend," or, "I'm staying on the couch."

This type of transient living arrangement used to be a huge problem for educators, because the student would be at a school for two weeks. Then they'd be gone for a month; then they'd be there for two months; then they'd be gone for a week; then they'd come for a day; then they'd be gone for two weeks; then they would be tested on that teacher's ability to teach and communicate.

Thankfully, the Federal McKinney-Vento Act of 1987 was expanded several years ago to allow kids experiencing homelessness to stay at the last school they were enrolled in when they first became homeless. It also requires the school district to provide transportation free of charge to and from their home school, regardless of what district the family resides in. In addition,

> Education is one of the equalizers for kids living in poverty

it requires schools to register homeless children, even if they don't have the normally required documents, like immunization records or proof of residence. The idea is that these kids will at least have one stable environment in their lives -- their school. The McKinney-Vento Act has proven to be very successful, even though it does cost additional money. Education is one of the equalizers for kids living in poverty as it provides a degree of stability, predictability, and services in an unstable environment.[34]

What Outcome Would You Expect?

Let's ponder a question together. Given Sara's family tree and these dynamics taking place in her home growing up, where would you expect Sara to end up as an adult? Maybe an addict, or in jail, or on the streets, or maybe a teenage mom? These are some of the possible outcomes one might expect based on the environment of generational poverty that Sara grew up in. But Sara is actually an exception to what you might expect. In fact, Sara, Neal, and Jenny are all exceptions. For Sara, school became a stable safe place where she excelled and did really well. She went on to college, got scholarships, put herself through college, and actually graduated with more money than she started with. How many of us could say that? Then, she got a job as a teller at a bank and worked her way up to being one of the top bankers. After the birth of her first child, she decided she wanted to help kids who were like herself. So Sara went back to school and became a teacher.

Sara's half brother, Neal, knew that college wasn't the right fit for him. After graduating from high school, Neal learned how to weld and got jobs working in the oil industry. He makes a very good living and has a stable living environment. And Sara's sister, Jenny, who received the most abuse for the longest amount of time of any of the kids, graduated at the top of her High School class. So, how is it possible with the environment these kids grew up in that they were able to be so successful? Relationships.

Each of the children had people outside of their family that poured into them. Some of those people were believers who took the time to be kind for kids in need. Some where teachers who showed the kids that they cared. Some where relatives that provided a safe place when there was nowhere else to go. Some were co-workers and bosses that provided friendship and opportunities to learn and grow.

The Impact of What We Do

Let's draw some practical points from Sara's story. First, change happens slowly. When working on these types of generational poverty issues the results may not be seen for a long

> Generational poverty is rarely solved overnight.

time. Generational poverty is rarely solved overnight. The people you interact with and serve may not realize the impact you are making for them until years later. For instance, Sara doesn't even remember the name of the teacher that cared for her, but she does remember how she made her feel. Sara is a teacher today because of a careing teacher more than 30 years ago. It takes time, so don't expect generational change to happen overnight.

As Christians, our time horizon needs to be long. Even generations long. As I've mentioned before, I run an emergency shelter for families experiencing homelessness. When we plan as a staff, I challenge my staff to think long term by asking, "What if one of the kids in the shelter was to write us a letter 15 years from now? What would we want it to say?"

Second, complex issues are rarely solved with one size fits all simple solutions. Serving marginalized people, who Jesus referred to as "the least of these," isn't a cookie cutter kind of thing. We're dealing with people who have complex issues developed over a long period of time. The resident's of Middle Classburg, love simple answers and efficient solutions. So we are constantly making solutions to solve poverty like we are making widgets on an assembly line. So we say things like, "If they would just…" or "If you follow my three steps to success…" However, solutions to poverty usually require messy relationships and can take a long time to develop. For example, do you know when the best time to intervene is to prevent a kid from dropping out of high school? When that child is in the third grade. The kids who get an intervention between 3rd and 6th grade are likely to get through 10th grade, and if they make it through 10th grade, they are likely to graduate. So what does a drop out intervention look like? One hour a week spent with a mentor -- someone like you and it usually does not involve a lot of tutoring, rather it's often just building a trusted relationship with a kid that will last from third grade until high school graduation.

Relationships the Essential Ingredient

Often as we set up social service programs or ministries we focus on the stuff we can provide, rather than the people in need. This is a key distinction because when we do this it's like a hospital pre-prescribing that everyone who enters the ER gets a cast on their arm. So what about the people with head injuries or heart attacks or anything other than a broken arm? Their needs do not get met. That sounds crazy, but this is exactly how we often treat missions and social services. Essentially we say, this is the thing we provide, rather than discovering the need of the person and working to help them with that need. The key ingredient to the most successful programs is relationships. In fact, rarely do the most successful guests coming out of my shelter programs say that the program was the thing that helped them the most. More often, they mention a staff member by name and what that person did for them, how they made them feel. It's about relationships.

Reflecting and Looking Ahead

1. Reflecting on this chapter, what did you learn about families living in poverty that will change how you relate to them in the future, both personally and in a ministry context?

2. In this chapter, We pointed out that "the communities of Povertyville, USA, are often built around matriarchal households." How have you seen or experienced this to be true? What has been the impact of matriarchal family structures on your own church or ministry?

3. What was your response to the story about the "irresponsible kid"? What kind of assumptions and snap judgments have you made about people who are struggling, only to discover you were wrong because you didn't know their full story? Discuss how we as Christians can do a better job of building relationships to understand people struggling in poverty.

For Additional Study
For additional individual or group study, including a more in-depth look at what Scripture teaches on this topic, see the Study Guide for this book.

The Ghetto, the Garden and the Gospel

Part 2 - The Garden

The Ghetto, the Garden and the Gospel

8
What Causes Poverty?

"Then God said, 'Let us make man in our image, after our likeness. And let them have dominion over the fish of the sea and over the birds of the heavens and over the livestock and over all the earth and over every creeping thing that creeps on the earth.' So God created man in his own image, in the image of God he created him; male and female he created them. And God blessed them. And God said to them, 'Be fruitful and multiply and fill the earth and subdue it, and have dominion over the fish of the sea and over the birds of the heavens and over every living thing that moves on the earth' . . . And God saw everything that he had made, and behold, it was very good." (Genesis 1:26-31)

Four Common Causes and Cures

Now, it's time to ask the really difficult question: What causes poverty? Up to this point we've discussed the symptoms of poverty, the kinds of things you and I see in Povertyville, USA. What we haven't discussed is what creates poverty. Where does poverty come from? These questions are profound and important to try and answer, because without identifying it will be nearly impossible to find effective solutions. Just as a doctor tries to identify the cause of an ailment so he or she can prescribe an effective treatment, we need to identify the cause of poverty so we can prescribe the right treatment.

Contemporary research on poverty, as reflected in most books on the subject, tends to focus on four common schools of thought concerning the causes of poverty and how to respond to those causes. While we will compare these with what the Bible has to say about the cause of poverty later, let me briefly describe each of these schools of thought.

1. <u>Poverty Is the Result of Poor Choices</u>: The first school of thought says that people are poor because they've made poor choices. People displaying this school of thought might say things like, "Well if they would just get off drugs…," or, "If they would just get a job…" For them, the idea is that poverty is really a personal behavioral issue. This is probably the most common perspective expressed by Americans concerning those in poverty. I believe this has to do with the manifest destiny, "pull yourself up by your bootstraps" mentality that persists in the U.S. It's part of our cultural identity that, if there is something wrong, then there is something wrong with you. This means that,

to fix the problem, you have to fix you. Maybe this is why self-help workshops, books, and articles are so numerous, popular, and why the self-help industry had an estimated value of $41.2 Billion in 2023.

So for those that think poor choices and bad decisions are the cause of poverty, what are their proposed solutions going to look like? Behavior modification, of course! Let's work with people to modify their behavior. Let's replace bad behavior with good behavior, poor choices with good ones. Since the problem is your behavior, you just need to fix how you behave. How do we do that? We set up programs that practice behavior modification, things like AA, parenting classes, or money management and budgeting classes. We set up processes and programs designed to modify an individual's bad behavior and to teach him or her good behavior.

> Since the problem is your behavior, you just need to fix how you behave.

2. Poverty Is the Result of a Lack of Resources: The second school of thought argues that the cause of poverty isn't poor decisions but inequality, which results in a lack of resources in the community. The idea here is that the problem isn't with the individual, but with the community and those who are hoarding resources. If inequality and a lack of resources is the root cause of poverty, what would you expect the proposed solutions would look like? Redistribution of resources, of course. How do we do that? By creating programs like the United Way, or most non-profits. We'll take resources from one group (donors) and redistribute them to another group (the poor).

> The problem isn't with the individual but with the community and those who are hoarding resources.

The thought here is that by redistributing resources we will create a more equitable society and reduce the community ills that create the conditions for bad behavior.

3. Poverty Is the Result of Exploitation: The third school of thought is that poverty is a result of exploitation or abuse and includes a whole raft of different things: predatory lenders (think payday loans and pawn shops in poor neighborhoods), human trafficking (including prostitution and sex trafficking),

drug trafficking, unfair labor practices, rent gouging slum landlords, and many others. For those that think exploitation is a root cause of poverty, their proposed solutions look like legislation and law enforcement. The idea being that we can legislate and enforce our laws to alleviate poverty. Additionally, we're going to vote and elect people to power who will focus on these things. Since the COVID19 Pandemic, we have seen a slew of new legislation across the US focused on homeless encampment enforcement, rent stabilization, and increased minimum wage and benefit requirements. Many of which would fit into this category.

4. Poverty Is the Result of Poor Government and Economic Systems: The fourth school of thought on the cause of poverty has to do with bad government or bad economic systems that are suppressing a group or that are keeping people poor. Examples of this could be Apartheid in South Africa, disenfranchisement of people groups in other countries, or in the US you will hear people that espouse this view say things like, welfare is trapping people in poverty. For those with this view their solutions are political activism, voting in a better government, pushing lawsuits against the government in the courts, or policing the governments of the world by creating a bigger government such as the United Nations or the World Bank. You may have seen videos of the United Nations convening on how they are going to enact penalties or embargoes on certain countries for their actions on specific people groups. Whereas, the United Nations tends act like the police the World Bank tends to act as an incentive for good government behaviors. This is actually an area where a lot of money is spent around the world. For example, in 2022 alone, the World Bank made commitments in excess of $115 Billion. Their mission is to end extreme poverty and boost shared prosperity on a livable planet. They do so by providing loans to countries that need them with requirements for certain government actions to remain in compliance with the loan and to have the ability to get future loans.

Toward a Biblical Understanding of Poverty

The four commonly offered causes of poverty, which we've looked at, all have defenders and all contain some degree of truth. However, whether taken alone or in combination, they all fall short of explaining the cause of the disease of poverty or how to cure it.

Perceived Causes	Attempted Cures
Poor Individual Behavior	Modify Behavior
Lack of Community Resources	Redistribute Resources
Exploitation	Laws & Enforcement
Poor Government or Economic Systems	Govern The Government

A biblical understanding of poverty begins with God, a man, a woman, and a Garden where everything in it is "good." Therefore, as Christians, we need to ask another question: What does the Bible have to say about the cause of poverty? To answer that question, and to get a Biblical perspective on people and poverty, we need to go all the way back to the beginning, to the first two chapters of Genesis. In Genesis, chapters one and two, we read how God creates the heavens and the earth. We learn that He creates everything in it, and He declares that all those things are "good." Then, God creates man and woman and says that they, too, are very good (Genesis 1:31). In addition to creating the man and the woman, and placing them in the Garden of Eden, God gives both the man and the woman jobs to do. To the man God assigns him with the task of tending and caring for the garden (Genesis 2:15-20). Specifically, God tells Adam that he's responsible for naming all the animals. Even today, this tendency to organize and categorize the world around us seems kind of innate to men. We name things. We categorize. We organize. The human race has this drive and ability which sets us apart from all other animals. We're driven to put things in order, to create categories, and to name things.

> A biblical understanding of poverty begins with God, a man, a woman, and a Garden where everything in it is "good."

What Causes Poverty?

Even my children argue about the proper name or category of something, which they always seem to do in the back seat of the car. "No, that dog is a chocolate lab, not a brown lab!" or, "No, the Pokemon is a legendary!" or, "No, dad is the best..." (Ok, well, maybe not the last one. They are Mama's boys!). Anyhow, the point is we categorize things, and doing so is important to humans. If you think about it, the core of Scientific exploration is to identify, name and describe natural phenomena in the world and universe around us. Secondly, God gives the woman the job of helping the man in this task. Additionally, together they were to be fruitful and to multiply. This is what God gives them at this point in history. God gave them work to do. And it, too, is good.

The story of mankind—the history of the human race—began in a garden. In that pristine beginning, there were no disparities of any kind, no socio-economic divisions. Yet, there was work to be done, and it was fulfilling. A quick note: if you think work is a curse, think again.

> We feel a profound sense of self-worth when we engage in meaningful work.

There will be work in heaven! Why? Because even in the perfection of the garden, God had tasks for us. He has embedded this desire to work and be productive so deeply within us that it elicits an emotional response. We feel a profound sense of self-worth when we engage in meaningful work. It provides dignity, purpose, and fulfillment. Poverty, on the other hand, strips this away.

This innate need to work and be productive is so important that we've incorporated it into what we do at the family shelter which I oversee. One of our core values, which guides our decision-making, is to be empowering toward our guests. The way this plays out in the day-to-day operation of the shelter is that our guests actually do most of the work at the shelter. We call these "service opportunities." You might call them chores. Our guests sign up to do things like mop the kitchen or do laundry (or something like that). Simple things like working in the kitchen to cook a meal or to clean up after dinner are incredibly therapeutic for a homeless mom. The result is that we see a profound change in people's demeanors just by doing something small like a kitchen chore. Why? Because work is important. To be able to do something, get it done, and help somebody else, is a big thing, particularly for people who are always on the receiving end.

I remember one single mother who was experiencing homelessness with her two children, who would sign up to mop the kitchen every night. One night I walked into the kitchen and saw her mopping away. I asked her, "Why do you always sign up to mop?" Her answer reverberates in my mind. She said, "I spend most of my day feeling like a failure. I can't give my kids a home. I can't solve my problems in a day, but I can mop this floor. It has a start and an end and I know when it is done. Also, it is the one chance I have for a little quiet each day."

This desire for productive work has been woven by God into the fabric of what it means to be human. Imagine always being on the begging end. Always feeling like you have to tell your most traumatic story over and over again in order to get some help. But, then you get the opportunity to give back and to serve. Suddenly there's a noticeable change in your demeanor. This desire for productive work has been woven by God into the fabric of what it means to be human, and it stretches all the way back to the beginning and God's assignment of productive work in the Garden of Eden.

> This desire for productive work has been woven by God into the fabric of what it means to be human.

All too often, what we have done in ministry and mission is create programs which basically say, "I'm gonna give you something," rather than, "Here's how you can get involved and give back." And, sometimes, the result is dependency rather than dignity. It's a painful reality that we may be hurting people more than we're helping them -- killing them (and their self-respect) with our kindness.

From the Garden to the Ghetto

We began this chapter with a question: What causes poverty? Up to this point, we've briefly considered the major competing schools of thought. We've also offered a brief overview of the creation account, which tells us that there was a time in human history when there were no disparities, when poverty didn't exist, and when there was good work to be done. The question hanging in the air is this: What happened? How did we get from the garden to the ghetto?

What Causes Poverty?

Reflecting and Looking Ahead

1. Reflecting on this chapter, what did you learn about the four common explanations offered for the causes of poverty that you didn't know before?

2. The four common explanations of poverty contain a certain degree of truth. What did you find yourself agreeing with? What did you disagree with? Explain.

3. Take a moment and reflect on the four common explanations of poverty. Before you studied this chapter, which of these four suggested causes would you have most agreed with? Has your thinking changed? What do you see as the difference between a cause of poverty and a symptom of something else? Give an example of a symptom verses a cause.

For Additional Study

For additional individual or group study, including a more in-depth look at what Scripture teaches on this topic, see the Study Guide for this book.

The Ghetto, the Garden and the Gospel

9

From The Garden To The Ghetto

"For the creation waits with eager longing for the revealing of the sons of God. For the creation was subjected to futility, not willingly, but because of him who subjected it, in hope that the creation itself will be set free from its bondage to corruption and obtain the freedom of the glory of the children of God. For we know that the whole creation has been groaning together in the pains of childbirth until now." (Romans 8:19-22)

In the previous chapter, we briefly reviewed the four standard theories for the causes of poverty and the responses those theories generate. Next, we began looking at the biblical story of creation. We ended the chapter with a question hanging in the air: *What happened? How did we get from the garden to the ghetto?* Now, it's time to answer that question.

Ground Zero: the Fall and its Effects

When we look at the beginning of things in Genesis 1 and 2, we see that God created everything and that everything He created was "very good" (Genesis 1:31). There was no disparity -- personally, socially, or economically. God tells the man and the woman that they have free reign to tend this beautiful place, this garden -- just don't do this one thing. Don't eat the fruit from that one tree because, if you do that, you'll know good and evil.

> "And the LORD God commanded the man, saying, 'You may surely eat of every tree of the garden, but of the tree of the knowledge of good and evil you shall not eat, for in the day that you eat of it you shall surely die'."(Genesis 2:16-17)

What neither of them realized was that they already knew good; they just didn't know evil. That would change.

We don't know how much time elapsed before evil invaded perfection, but when it happened it came in the form of a serpent. "Now the serpent was more crafty than any other beast of the field that the LORD God had made. He said to the woman, 'Did God actually say, "You shall not eat of any tree in the garden'?" (Genesis 3:1).

The Ghetto, the Garden and the Gospel

The serpent tempted Eve, who ate the fruit of the forbidden tree and gave it to her husband, who also ate it. It's difficult to find words to adequately describe the spiritual, moral, and practical catastrophe that unfolded on that day. In an instant, everything changed, with ripple effects you and I continue to experience today. If you want a biblical understanding of when, where, and how poverty started, drive a stake in the ground right here in Genesis 3. Theologians call it "the Fall" and it is ground zero for understanding poverty. Everything you and I understand as poverty, in its many expressions, started here. Sin entered the world, and the effects of it would bring both spiritual poverty and tangible physical poverty to all of humankind.

> Theologians call it "the Fall" and it is ground zero for understanding poverty.

Suddenly, in that moment of profound spiritual failure, things the man and woman had never known before came sweeping over them like a flood. Shame. Guilt. Fear. Separation from each other. And, worst of all, separation from their Creator. "Then the eyes of both were opened, and they knew that they were naked. And they sewed fig leaves together and made themselves loincloths." (Genesis 3:7) In what we can only understand as an act of profound mercy and love, God came looking for His wayward creature:

> "And they heard the sound of the LORD God walking in the garden in the cool of the day, and the man and his wife hid themselves from the presence of the LORD God among the trees of the garden. But the LORD God called to the man and said to him, 'Where are you?'" (Genesis 3:8-9)

I have no doubt that God knew exactly where Adam and Eve were, but they were hiding because they were suddenly confronted by all of their new-found issues. Isn't that how you and I respond when we're confronted with our sin and issues to this day? We feel shame. We feel guilt. We feel afraid. We realize that our real selves are exposed. So, we hide. We hide from God and we hide from others. We can't let other's know we are broken. So even after all the centuries which have rolled by since that terrible day in the garden, we as humans still have this same basic response that kicks in when our sin and brokenness overwhelm us. We hide.

In cultures of poverty, particularly where children have traumatic experiences and multiple care-givers early in childhood, this hiding response can become ingrained into behavioral patterns and impact relationships throughout life. Sometimes diagnosed as attachment disorders, it manifests itself in responses to stressors: *I'm going to wall up. I'm not going to let others in. I'm going to become distant, tough, independent so others won't know the real me and therefore, will not be able to hurt or reject me.* It's a defense mechanism that says, *I want to be loved, but I don't want you to get too close.* As a result, there's a push-and-pull dynamic that enters into relationships with broken people living in Povertyville, USA. Think of it as an emotional dance, where one partner pulls the other person close with one arm, but with the other arm pushes their partner away. This often causes an emotional roller coaster effect and inhibits close, secure relationships from forming. Along with this playing out in marriage relationships, you will often see this when you are involved in orphan care, are foster or adoptive parents, or when you are counseling people from poverty backgrounds.[35] Just like Adam and Eve, when confronted with sin, those that come from insecure relational connections as children often hide their emotions. All of us have a tendency to hide.

Curses and Broken Relationships

God's response to the man and the woman is as profound as the choices which brought them to this point. He issues a series of curses. While that may sound harsh to our ears, we need to remember that curses are simply God's formal declaration of the consequences for our choices and actions. And He begins with the serpent:

> "The LORD God said to the serpent, 'Because you have done this, cursed are you above all livestock and above all beasts of the field; on your belly you shall go, and dust you shall eat all the days of your life. I will put enmity between you and the woman, and between your offspring and her offspring; he shall bruise your head, and you shall bruise his heel'." (Genesis 3:14-15)

The Ghetto, the Garden and the Gospel

Next, God turns His attention to the woman, declaring, "I will surely multiply your pain in childbearing; in pain you shall bring forth children. Your desire shall be contrary to your husband, but he shall rule over you"(Genesis 3:16). What should have been the joy of childbirth and the raising of children would now be a blessing mixed with both physical and emotional pain. Anyone who has raised kids understands this truth in a way that defies description.

God seems to reserve His most severe response for the man:

> "And to Adam he said, 'Because you have listened to the voice of your wife and have eaten of the tree of which I commanded you, 'You shall not eat of it,' cursed is the ground because of you; in pain you shall eat of it all the days of your life; thorns and thistles it shall bring forth for you; and you shall eat the plants of the field. By the sweat of your face you shall eat bread, till you return to the ground, for out of it you were taken; for you are dust, and to dust you shall return'." (Genesis 3:17-19)

A lot of ink has been spilled over the years by interpreters writing on this passage. We'll confine ourselves to some basic observations which have immediate relevance to our understanding of poverty and its cause.

First, work existed prior to the Fall, Adam and Eve had jobs to do in tending to the garden and helping on another and that work was good. Apparently it also was not hard until this point. Creation didn't resist man's efforts to tend the garden. Now, after the Fall and God's response, there's still work, but a profound change has taken place. Good work has now become hard toil. Creation now resists man's efforts. From this point forward, sweat, tears and pain will be involved in man's work to survive and tend Creation.

Second, mankind was designed to work. We have within us the characteristics of the creator himself. We can gain deep satisfaction from our work, but at the same time work is hard. So we, as humans, need work, meaningful work that produces fruit.

Third, because work becomes hard the Fall opens the door for disparity to enter the world. Differences emerge, differences between those who have and those who have not, between those who want to keep and others who want to take. We no longer are in a perfect garden where all of our needs are met and we have all things in common. Rather, differences emerge quickly. So quickly in fact, that in one generation the children of Adam and Eve -- Cain and Abel -- kill over their disparities (Genesis 4).

A Broken Relationship with God [36]

The Fall at its core creates a rift, a tear in the fabric of relationships. At this point there is profound brokenness in man's relationship with God, in his relationships with other humans, and in his relationship with creation itself. The ripple effects of man's Fall into sin roll out through time, touching everything and everyone, and cause continued fractures in our relationships right up to today.

The Fall Causes and Sin Perpetuates Broken Relationships

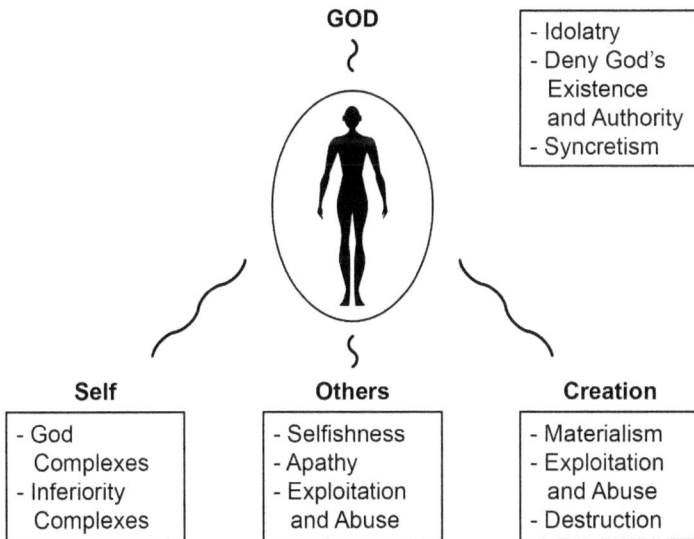

GOD

- Idolatry
- Deny God's Existence and Authority
- Syncretism

Self
- God Complexes
- Inferiority Complexes

Others
- Selfishness
- Apathy
- Exploitation and Abuse

Creation
- Materialism
- Exploitation and Abuse
- Destruction

The first relationship that breaks is our relationship with God. The fractures in our relationship with God tend to play out in three primary ways: idolatry, atheism and syncretism. Where man's relationship with God in the garden was close and intimate, we now have become idolatrous. In fact, the serpent's temptation of Eve was in fact this very sin. If we were in control we could be like God and we would not need to follow or submit to him because we would be in control. You may think, I am not idolatrous, because I have never worshiped a golden calf and I don't really have a high view of myself either. However, idolatry is found when we focusing our hearts and affections on anything that compromises our dependence upon God and our willingness to surrender our will to His will. Idolatry happens when we believe we know better than God how to handle a situation. If you truly think about it, is there anything in your life that you would hold back and not allow God to take from you? As a parent, I can honestly say, that I have a hard time trusting my children and their future to anyone, including God. That is my idolatry. It is when we say, "Okay God, you can have everything else in my life, but you can't have this one thing. I'm going to do this thing my way." That is idolatry. When it comes to understanding poverty in our Western culture, one of the most widespread forms of idolatry can be found in materialism.

Materialism represents the strongest form of idolatry in Scripture -- one that worships the creation rather than the Creator (Romans 1:24-25). On the issue of poverty, the four commonly offered explanations of poverty,

> Materialism represents the strongest form of idolatry in Scripture.

along with their solutions, are all rooted in materialism. They send the message that we don't need God's help to solve poverty. If we just change man's material situation, poverty will be eliminated. According to materialism, man actually does live by bread alone. The biblical explanation of poverty is different, because it's rooted in man's relationship with God. The biblical worldview recognizes the material reality of poverty, but it also recognizes man's need for something greater. Therefore, any solution to poverty must involve the whole person, both materially and spiritually.

The second fracture we see in our broken relationship with God is atheism. Atheism means "no god" and is the denial of God's very existence. Not just a worship of the creation rather than the Creator, but an outright denial that there is or ever was a creator in the first place. If God does not exist then we can do whatever we want, to whomever we want, however we want.

Finally, if idolatry means worshiping the wrong god, and if atheism means worshiping no god, then syncretism means worshiping a mixed-up god. Our English word "syncretism" comes from a Greek word meaning "to mix together." Syncretism means that we mix biblical truth with things which are incompatible with clear biblical teachings. Writing in The Exchange for *Christianity Today* online, Ed Stetzer defines religious syncretism as:

> "the mixing of Christianity with something else such that they become a different gospel. Syncretism can take place with a positive-thinking gospel, a nationalist emphasis, or emerging culture. Syncretism happens more than we might know."[37]

By now you may be thinking, so what if our broken relationship with God causes idolatry, atheism or syncretism? What difference does it make? Well, the answer is that all of these take God from His rightful place, both as Creator and as the One with authority to determine how His creation is to be used. They all replace God with something else, usually something that can be controlled or manipulated by man. If man can control it, then he will misuse it. I have two boys, and my boys have never seen their mother or me make a weapon and harm the other. But the second my boys have anything in their hands, whether it's a stick, a rock, or socks, they inevitably find a way to use that new tool as a weapon against the other. Yep, just junior versions of Cain and Abel! Once one of us thinks we're in control, then everything and everyone exists for me. That's why these broken views of God matter. They eventually manifest themselves in other broken relationships.

A Broken Relationship with Ourselves

If we see God wrong, then we will see ourselves wrong, too. So, the next relationship that breaks as a result of the Fall is our relationship with ourselves and our view of ourselves. This break usually takes us in one of two directions.

The first direction is to go to the extreme of "everything's about me." This direction of our brokenness produces a superiority complex. Some people call this a "god complex."

If we see God wrong, then we will see ourselves wrong, too.

The Ghetto, the Garden and the Gospel

Whether we would say it or not, when we act out of a superiority complex we demand control. We say things like, "if you would just…" or "if they would just…" or we get angry when things are not done exactly how we would want them done. We could also call this the "invictus complex," named after the poem "Invictus" by the English poet, William Ernest Henley, who wrote:

"It matters not how strait the gate,
How charged with punishments the scroll,
I am the master of my fate,
I am the captain of my soul."

The other direction this break can take is to the opposite extreme of developing an inferiority complex. When operating from an inferiority complex we feel that we have no control. Everything is done to us, no matter what we want or do. Let's pause and ask a question that brings this discussion back to the issue of understanding poverty. Which of these two directions do you think each of the three categories of people (Poverty, Middle Class, Wealth) tend to move toward? Middle class and wealth tend to move toward the superiority complex, while people in poverty tend toward the inferiority complex. This is super important to recognize because most Christian mission work tends to reinforce these broken views of ourselves. We tend to come into an impoverished community with our mission teams and we say, "Here's what your problem is, and here's how we're going to fix it." To the people in that community they hear again and again, there is a problem with you and if you do what this other person says then you can get the stuff they can provide. The net effect is that we actually worsen the gap in broken relationships by the way we approach missions and by the way we engage with the people we want to help. Most mission work and most people that do this work truly do want to serve and help, but the problem is that it has been ingrained into those in Middle Class and Wealth that we have to do and achieve. So we tend to setup projects and programs that treat people in need like they are widgets moving down a conveyor belt. You can tell when this has happened when the measurement for success is some output. How many meals did we serve? How many coats did we give away? Etc. Rather the focus should be on life change, both yours and theirs. How we do what we do matters, more than what we do.

A Broken Relationship with Others

If we see God wrong, and we see ourselves wrong, then we will see others wrong, too. The next broken relationship from the Fall is man's relationship with other men. This broken relationship between men (and women) frequently fractures in one of three ways.

> If we see God wrong, and we see ourselves wrong, then we will see others wrong.

First, it creates things like selfishness. I just want it my way. I don't care about what happens to you or anyone else. As a result, we If we see God wrong, and we see ourselves wrong, then we will see others wrong. This can be seen in children from the time they are infants. Children will take things from other children and cry if they don't get what they want. As every parent knows, one of the early words in a child's vocabulary is, "Mine!"

The *second* fracture appears in the form of apathy. We may not fully reach a point of saying, "I really don't care," but we express our apathy in other ways. For example, we may "like" something on Social Media, but we don't really care about it. Come on, you've done it. There's this big thing going viral on Facebook and you want to feel like you're a part of it. So, you click the "like" button. But you don't really care about that thing or the people involved. Sometimes it's even called compassion fatigue. I am too tired or too focused on something else to care about the suffering of others, their pain, or what's happening in the world.

There's a *third* fracture generated by our brokenness with others: the outright exploitation of others. Selfishness and apathy have turned to callousness, allowing humans to exploit and abuse others. This response can express itself in things like drug dealing, engaging in sex trafficking, or being involved in predatory lending. Selfishness and apathy have turned to callousness, allowing humans to exploit and abuse others.

It can be any number of things we know are not right, but we're going to do them anyway because it's about my gain, regardless of their pain. I just don't care if it hurts someone else. I've had people defend their actions of

> Selfishness and apathy have turned to callousness, allowing humans to exploit and abuse others.

exploiting others by saying, "So what? It's a dog eat dog world. I'm going to get mine." This kind of sentiment is an expression that I no longer care about anyone else, and I'm willing to engage in the outright exploitation or abuse of others.

A Broken Relationship with Creation

All of these broken relationships lead to a broken relationship between man and God's creation. The Bible talks about this brokenness, telling us, "For we know that the whole creation has been groaning together in the pains of childbirth until now" (Romans 8:22). If we see God wrong . . . we will also see God's creation wrongly. Because of our broken relationship with God and His creation, we have become materialistic. Materialism is both a form of idolatry (worshiping the creation, rather than the Creator), and a form of abuse against God's creation. He created the world to be enjoyed, not exploited or abused. Materialism says it doesn't matter what happens to the world around us. We're just going to take what we can for ourselves. We're going to focus on today and not worry about the future. We're going to get ours and forget about our community. We're going to use up all the resources in an area no matter what happens to it, and then we're going to move on. We're going to break things down, mess things up, and we're not going to make any effort to repair the damage we've done. Materialism inevitably results in the exploitation, abuse, and, ultimately, the destruction of what has been entrusted to us.

The effects of the Fall and the entry of sin into God's perfect creation have been profound, on-going, and long lasting. They reach across time to touch us all. We see them every day in the world around us. And we experience them in every broken relationship. Such a profound disease requires an equally profound cure. Thankfully, one has been provided. And that's where we need to go next.

Reflecting and Looking Ahead

1. Reflecting on this chapter, what did you learn about the Fall and its effects that you didn't know before? How does what you learned impact your understanding of poverty?

2. Chapter 9 began with the question, "What happened? How did we get from 'the garden to the ghetto'?" Based on what you learned in this chapter, how would you answer that question?

3. How is Genesis chapter 3 "ground zero" for our understanding of poverty and its many manifestations?

For Additional Study

For additional individual or group study, including a more in-depth look at what Scripture teaches on this topic, see the Study Guide for this book.

The Ghetto, the Garden and the Gospel

10
The Cause And The Cure

"Therefore, as one trespass led to condemnation for all men, so one act of righteousness leads to justification and life for all men." (Romans 5:18)

Let's do a quick review before plunging ahead. In chapter 8, we looked at the four most common schools of thought concerning the causes of Poverty. Next, in chapter 9, we looked at the biblical narrative of creation and the fall of man into sin. We said that if you and I want a biblical understanding of when, where, and how poverty started, we need to drive a stake in the ground in Genesis 3, because the events of that chapter represent ground zero for understanding poverty. Now it's time to tie the causes presented in the last two chapters together and then move on to the cure.

Poverty and its Cause

Reflecting on the commonly offered explanations for poverty, along with what we learned from Genesis 3, we're forced to ask a question: Is poverty simply the result of poor individual behavior and bad personal choices?

> Spiritually speaking, we all live in some part of "the Ghetto."

Or are the four common explanations actually symptoms of something much deeper than bad choices about how people living in Povertyville, USA, manage their money? Could this mean that those of us living in Middle Classburg, America, share with our relatives in Povertyville a type of poverty that's not necessarily financial in nature, but spiritual? Beginning with the Fall in Genesis 3, the ripple effects of that spiritual catastrophe roll down through the generations and across all socio-economic classes. Those ripple effects impact us in Middle Classburg just as much as they impact the residents of Povertyville, as they continue to roll over all of us and create disparities which eventually result in poverty. The ripple effects of the Fall, those disparities and the poverty they produce, are all part of what I call the Ghetto. Spiritually speaking, we all live in some part of the Ghetto.

Poverty is a result of the Fall and so are Middle Class and Wealth. Before the

Fall, none of those divisions, disparities, or classes existed. This means within each economic class there exists both good and brokenness. We are all impacted by the Fall and therefore none of us get to escape its effects, no matter the size of our bank accounts. As Christians, our goal isn't to make poor people into Middle Class people, but to make all people into God's people. We want to see all people reconciled and their brokenness healed no matter their socio-economic status.

> We are all impacted by the Fall and therefore none of us get to escape its effects, no matter the size of our bank accounts.

Bad choices and poor individual behavior are the result of personal sin and brokenness. A lack of resources within the community caused by the hoarding of resources is another ripple effect of sin. Our sin manifests in selfishness and creates a desire to hold on to what we have, rather than sharing and using it to meet needs and solve problems. This brokenness results in exploitation or abuse, which are also sins. All of these issues (and many more) are ultimately the result of our sin nature. All of these broken things, which we referred to earlier as causes of poverty, are actually symptoms of something much deeper. In order to address all of those symptoms, we have to begin by addressing the root cause. Otherwise, we're just modifying behavior, redistributing resources, and changing laws without real lasting change. Such steps might be helpful in the near term, but to reach a genuine long-term cure, the heart must change and our brokenness must be healed.

Poverty and its Cure

During the Jesus Movement of the 1970s, Christian performing artist Andrae Crouch taught Christians to sing, *"Jesus is the answer for the world today, above him there's no other, Jesus is the way."* It's a simple, biblical truth, and a deeply profound answer to the problem of healing man's brokenness and curing poverty. Yes, as Christians who take the Scriptures seriously, we believe that Jesus is the answer. If sin is a disease, then Jesus is the cure. Jesus embodies the culmination of God's plan for man's redemption and restoration, a plan which began immediately after man's Fall into sin in Genesis 3.

The Cause And The Cure

The entire biblical narrative traces God's plan as it unfolds throughout the centuries, offering us little glimpses along the way of what reconciliation and restoration might look like. Then, in the fullness of time, God sends His Son to intervene in our poverty and to restore our broken relationships, starting with our relationship with God. Jesus comes to the earth and begins His public ministry with a sermon in the Synagogue in Nazareth, taken from the Old Testament book of Isaiah:

> "And the scroll of the prophet Isaiah was given to him. He unrolled the scroll and found the place where it was written, 'The Spirit of the Lord is upon me, because he has anointed me to proclaim good news to the poor. He has sent me to proclaim liberty to the captives and recovering of sight to the blind, to set at liberty those who are oppressed, to proclaim the year of the Lord's favor.' And he rolled up the scroll and gave it back to the attendant and sat down. And the eyes of all in the synagogue were fixed on him. And he began to say to them, 'Today this Scripture has been fulfilled in your hearing'" (Luke 4:17-21).

Boom! Jesus Came to Proclaim Good News to the Poor!

Consider this the ultimate "mic-drop" moment, and it took place in a Synagogue in Nazareth some 2,000 years ago. That's right. Boom! Jesus came to proclaim good news to the poor! I often hear well-meaning Christians say, "Well, Jesus was talking about people who are spiritually poor, not people who are physically poor." That's only partly true. While it is true that Jesus said, "Blessed are the poor in spirit" (Matthew 5:3), Luke's account of Jesus' words leaves out the "in spirit" part and simply says, "Blessed are you who are poor" (Luke 6:20). This isn't a contradiction, but a reminder that Jesus' teaching on the subject should not be treated as an "either-or" choice, but as addressing both physical-economic poverty and poverty of spirit. Jesus also told the rich young ruler to sell all his possessions and give the money to the poor (Matthew 10:21). Jesus obviously wasn't talking about the "spiritually poor" in that passage. There's more. With Jesus, there always is.

Since Classical times, the Greek word for poor (*ptochos*) was the common Greek term for people who lived in absolute poverty -- beggars. Without violating the Greek sense, today we might call them panhandlers. It described people who were economically destitute. We find this word on the lips of Jesus when He describes His ministry for the messengers sent by John the Baptist, "And he answered them, 'Go and tell John what you have seen and heard: the blind receive their sight, the lame walk, lepers are cleansed, and the deaf hear, the dead are raised up, the poor have good news preached to them'" (Luke 7:22).

The physical condition of the poor in this passage is as real and tangible as the physical condition of the blind, the lame, the lepers, the deaf, and the dead. They are physically destitute. The same is true when Jesus describes the kind of people we should invite to our banquets (think church potluck): "But when you give a feast, invite the poor, the crippled, the lame, the blind" (Luke 14:13; and Luke 16:20). Finally, James uses this same word when he chastises his readers for discriminating against the poor in favor of the rich in their church gatherings (James 2:1-13). Jesus' ministry focused on the poor and the marginalized, as did the ministry of the early church.

Middle Class Jesus?

Growing up in Middle Classburg, America, most of us have a mental idea of a Middle Class Jesus. We have a tendency to see a man who had all His physical needs put together and was just teaching the Scripture like we see a lot of our own pastors and church leaders doing today. Even our images of Jesus show a man in gleaming white robes and long perfectly styled hair. However, if we take a moment and reflect on the reality of Jesus' life on Earth, we might find something quite different.

Jesus was born homeless to a teenage mom and he spent the first few years of His life as a refugee, fleeing government persecution and unable to return home. At some early point in Jesus' life, something happened to his father. We don't know the details or circumstances, but Joseph disappears from the biblical narrative sometime after Jesus turns twelve. When Jesus begins His ministry around the age of thirty, dad's not in the picture anymore. For the next three years or so, Jesus walks around with a group of young men that we would probably label a "gang" today. Let's face it. Today, someone would probably be calling the cops to report "Jesus and His gang" hanging out in the neighborhood and up to no good. Oh wait, that's kind of what happened in the Scripture, isn't it? At the close of His ministry, Jesus rides into town on a borrowed donkey, the transportation of a poor man and the fulfillment of a prophecy. He is sleeping outside, homeless, the night he was betrayed. He's abused by men of power and wealth and human-trafficked by a friend who betrays and sells Him for thirty pieces of silver. He is falsely accused and imprisoned. His accusers mock Him by putting princely robes on Him because His own clothes were so poor, and his Roman executioners cast lots and gamble for whatever is left over. Finally, Jesus is buried in a borrowed tomb. Jesus was too poor to die. Think about that. There are people in your community and mine today who, like Jesus, are too poor to die. Jesus lived the poor man's life.

So, here's the question. Does anything from Jesus' life suggest that He lived what we would call a Middle Class life? No! Jesus was a resident of Povertyville, and He spent most of His ministry time with people who lived there, too. In fact in Matthew 8:20 Jesus says, "Foxes have holes, and birds of the air have nests, but the Son of Man has nowhere to lay his head."

> Jesus was a resident of Povertyville and He spent most of His ministry time with people who lived there, too.

In a revealing and frankly terrifying postscript, during the last week of His ministry, Jesus takes the extraordinary step of saying that by serving the poor and marginalized ("the least of these"), we will be serving Him. And doing so or not doing so will have eternal consequences (Matthew 25:31-46). Our present dominant theological schools of thought both have trouble with this section of scripture because it states that how we serve the less fortunate will determine if we will be forever with God or forever separated from Him. This seems to simultaneously be in conflict with a school thought that says, "once saved always saved," while also challenging a school of thought that says God has predetermined who he would save. However, these are the red letter words of Jesus, so we have to do something with them.

The message is clear. God intends the reconciliation that He brings about in Jesus to impact how we treat others, especially the poor. That's what Jesus modeled. That's what the early church practiced. And that's what the church today needs to re-engage.

Reconciliation and New Ripple Effects [38]

When it comes to reconciliation and restoration, God initiates, and we follow. As Jesus described to Nicodemus in John 3, God's great love reconciles us by grace through faith and brings us into a right relationship with Him through Jesus Christ (Ephesians 2:8-10). Jesus called that moment of faith and reconciliation being "born again." As a result of our reconciliation with God and the restoration our relationship with Him, we begin to see things differently.

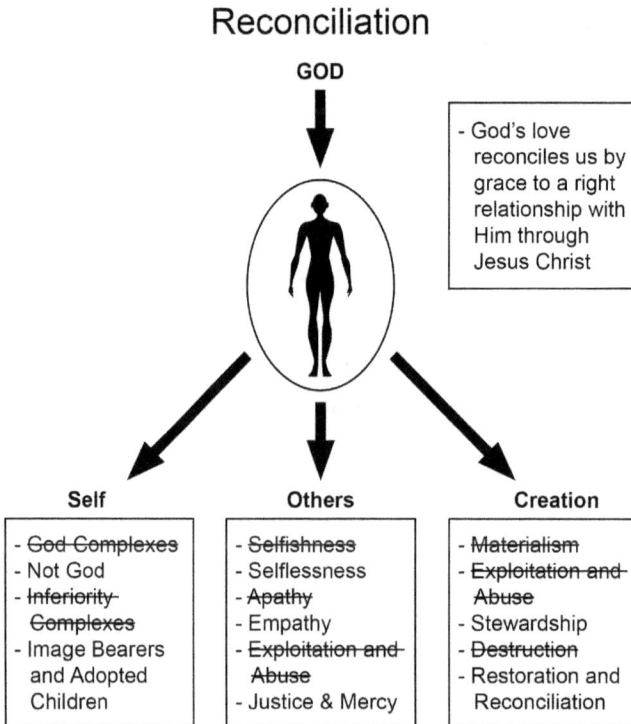

Reconciliation

GOD

- God's love reconciles us by grace to a right relationship with Him through Jesus Christ

Self	Others	Creation
- ~~God Complexes~~ - Not God - ~~Inferiority Complexes~~ - Image Bearers and Adopted Children	- ~~Selfishness~~ - Selflessness - ~~Apathy~~ - Empathy - ~~Exploitation and Abuse~~ - Justice & Mercy	- ~~Materialism~~ - ~~Exploitation and Abuse~~ - Stewardship - ~~Destruction~~ - Restoration and Reconciliation

New ripple effects begin to roll out through us. Once we see God rightly, we start to see ourselves rightly. I see that I'm not God, but I also see that I'm no longer inferior. I'm not God, but I have been made in the image of God, and so have you, and so have the people you and I are called to serve. I'm not superior or inferior. We're all here together as people who share the image of God. And because we all share His image, we all have value. Every life matters, because we all share His image.

This reality makes a profound difference in our ministry among the poor. When we walk into a ministry situation and say, "You're valuable. You've been made in the image of God. We both have something to teach each other. We have something to give back and forth," that new reality profoundly changes the way we do missions. For example, at the shelter where I serve, we don't refer to people as clients but as guests. And all of our guests participate with us as we work together on the issues which brought them to the shelter. We actually have them drive most of what takes place. We ask them questions. What do you need? What's your goal? How can we help? And here's how you can help us by improving this place, by serving around here, and by being great neighbors in our community.

As the ripple effects of reconciliation and restoration work their way through our lives, things begin to change. Mark Terrell is the founder and Spiritual Director at Cup of Cool Water, an outreach to teens experiencing

> How we see people is the beginning of how we treat people.

homelessness on the streets of Spokane, Washington. Mark teaches his staff and volunteers that, "How we see people is the beginning of how we treat people." How we see people is one of the things which changes as God's reconciliation takes hold of us, and we begin to see both ourselves and others as valuable people created in His image. As a result, what was selfishness is transformed into genuine selflessness. Suddenly, the spiritual scales fall from our eyes, and we begin to understand what the Apostle Paul really meant when he told the Ephesian elders at Miletus, "In all things I have shown you that by working hard in this way we must help the weak and remember the words of the Lord Jesus, how he himself said, 'It's more blessed to give than to receive'" (Acts 20:35).

Because we see differently, we give differently. Bad individual choices and behaviors change, and we begin taking care of others. Apathy becomes empathy. Rather than hoarding resources, we begin sharing and redistributing them. Why? Because now, I actually care about somebody else. I actually care about their situation. This is what happens as the reconciling work of Christ works its way in me, by the Holy Spirit, to restore the image of God that sin corrupted -- just as Paul told the Christian believers in Corinth, "But we all, with unveiled face beholding as in a mirror the glory of the Lord, are being transformed into the same image from glory to glory, just as from the Lord, the Spirit" (2 Corinthians 3:18 NASB).

As this spiritual process works its way out, apathy becomes empathy, while exploitation and abuse are replaced with a genuine desire to seek justice and mercy. These two -- justice and

> Our God is a God of both justice and mercy.

mercy -- present us with one of those biblical tensions which Scripture never fully resolves to our satisfaction. But unresolved Scriptural tensions often exist for an important reason: to prevent us from choosing one over the other, as if they somehow represent an "either-or" choice. They don't. These kinds of tensions remind us that God wants us to embrace "both-and." Our God is a God of both justice and mercy (Isaiah 30:18).

As God's reconciliation takes hold of us, it changes our relationship with His creation. Our former materialism, which led to exploitation and abuse, becomes transformed into an understanding of stewardship. We begin to understand that God has given each of us gifts, which He wants us to use to steward all of his other gifts, including creation: "As each has received a gift, use it to serve one another, as good stewards of God's varied grace" (1 Peter 4:10). Scripture teaches us that the world's resources belong to God, and we've been charged with stewarding, managing, and caring for what He's given us. As materialism gives way to an understanding of stewardship, our exploitation and abuse of God's creation gives way to a genuine concern for conservation. Rather than engaging in the wanton destruction of the world's resources, we embrace a genuine desire for restoration. We want to repair what's been broken, in our community, our society, and our world.

Finally, God's reconciliation in our lives has one more major impact on us. It transforms us into new creations. And that's where our discussion needs to go next.

Reflecting and Looking Ahead

1. Reflecting on this chapter, what one new thing did you learn about the causes of poverty?

2. Based on what you discovered in this chapter, what is the common spiritual connection between the residents of Middle Classburg, America, and the residents of Povertyville, USA? How does the biblical doctrine of the Fall help us explain the disparities between the various economic categories we've talked about in this book?

3. Discuss this statement from chapter 10, "As Christians, our goal isn't to make poor people into Middle Class people, but to make all people into God's people." Do you agree or disagree? How does our presentation of the gospel sometimes communicate a lot about our socio-economic status?

For Additional Study

For additional individual or group study, including a more in-depth look at what Scripture teaches on this topic, see the Study Guide for this book.

The Ghetto, the Garden and the Gospel

Part 3 - The Gospel

The Ghetto, the Garden and the Gospel

11

New Creations

"Therefore, if anyone is in Christ, he is a new creation. The old has passed away; behold, the new has come." (2 Corinthians 5:17)

Reconciliation and Transformation

In the previous section (Part 2 - The Garden), we looked at the true cause of poverty and the biblical cure. We discovered that mankind's Fall into sin is the ultimate cause of poverty, and that Jesus is the ultimate cure. Now, it's time to consider how the good news of Jesus transforms us and how it should transform how we see the world.

A popular Christian apologist was fond of saying that Jesus doesn't make bad people good. Jesus makes dead people live. Likewise, Jesus didn't come to make poor people into Middle Class people. Jesus came to make all people God's people. As Christians working to better understand man's journey from the Garden to

> Jesus didn't come to make poor people into Middle Class people. Jesus came to make all people God's people.

the Ghetto, and how the Gospel brings us into His Kingdom and leads us toward the City of God, our goal cannot be to make poor people into Middle Class people. It's not our highest goal to move the residents of Povertyville, USA, into Middle Classburg, America. Our highest goal is to see all people embrace the good news of the Gospel, to see them reconciled by faith, and to see their heart change dramatically alter their relationships with God, themselves, others and creation.

Reconciliation is the point in our lives where God's "spiritual light switch" flips, and the light of the Gospel shines on the reality that, as Christians, we're new creations with a new citizenship. Our old citizenship in Povertyville or Middle Classburg has passed away and has been replaced with a new citizenship in the Kingdom of God. "But our citizenship is in heaven, and from it we await a Savior, the Lord Jesus Christ" (Philippians 3:20). The Kingdom is your new home. This doesn't mean that we don't want to improve the living situation of those in need. Just the opposite. It means our reasoning and motivation behind why and how we serve others change. And when our motivation and our reasons change, how we go about serving others changes, too.

Our new citizenship in the Kingdom of God changes the way we see and understand everything else. We are no longer conformed to the things and ways of this world, and our transformation by the values of the Kingdom is now underway: "Do not be conformed to this world, but be transformed by the renewal of your mind, that by testing you may discern what is the will of God, what is good and acceptable and perfect." (Romans 12:2). As followers of Christ who have been reconciled to God in Christ, we're called to transform our thinking about how we interact with those in different socioeconomic classes. There are things that need to be reconciled in every socioeconomic class. The residents of Middle Classburg, America, need transformation just as much as their cousins in Povertyville, USA. As followers of Christ and as new creations with transformed minds, how we see the world needs to be transformed, too. Transformation means shifting from a worldly way of seeing and thinking, that often revolves around socioeconomic status, to a new way that revolves around what it means to be a new creation and a new citizen with a new citizenship in God's Kingdom.

Transformed Thinking

It's time now to look at specific ways that a transformed mind and transformed thinking impacts the way we understand issues of socioeconomic status. Earlier, in chapter 6, we looked at a chart entitled "Understanding Our Differences" which highlighted six key characteristics that tend to distinguish the residents of Middle Classburg, America, from the residents of

"The arc of the moral universe is long, but it bends toward justice."
Dr. Martin Luther King, Jr.

Povertyville, USA. What I didn't tell you then is there's another classification that we need to examine, and a third column we need to fill in. It's time to offer six biblical characteristics which we, as Christians and transformed people, should bring to this discussion. We'll begin filling in the chart in this chapter, and we'll complete it in the next chapter.

Understanding Our Differences			
Characteristic	Middle Class	Poverty	Christian
Time	Future	Present/Now	
Money	Manage/Save	Spend	
Worldview	City/Region	Ultra Local	
Emphasis	Quality	Quantity	
Driving Force	Achievement	Relationships	
Mental Model	Segmented Pizza	Ball of Yarn	

Time. We discovered earlier that for people living in Middle Classburg, America, their view of time is focused on the future. But, for those living in Povertyville, we learned that their view of time is focused on the present. For the residents of Povertyville, the time is always now. But where should the Christian view of time be focused? Our focus should be on Eternity. Our time focus should be the long view, the long arc of history. As Dr. Martin Luther King, Jr. once observed, "The arc of the moral universe is long, but it bends toward justice."[39] The reason why "the arc of the moral universe is long" is because it stretches into eternity and has its roots in the Kingdom of God.

As Christians, our eternal view of time has a practical impact. It means that our view of effective ministry has to look beyond a desire to quickly move people through a process or a program. We aren't making widgets, so if your ministry is only counting outputs (number of people served, meals handed out, coats donated) rather than outcomes (lives transformed) you probably have an error in how you view time.

Let me illustrate what I mean. I recently had an all-day training meeting with my staff at the family shelter I run. We started out talking about the number of families and kids we presently had in the shelter and how to get them to the next step out of the shelter. I suggested that we consider a different perspective. Instead of just thinking about how to get housing right now for these parents and their kids (although that need must be addressed), let's think about what we want their lives to be like fifteen years from now. What if, fifteen years from now, one of these kids who stayed with us was to write us a letter. What would we want that letter from one of these kids to say about their time here and how it changed their life? That's the long view. When you and I get to heaven, are we going to see one of these kids -- one of the people we helped in this life -- and what will they say about the time they spent with us?

This long-term, eternal perspective should impact our outreach work. It should help us understand that we may not see all the results of our efforts in the short-term. But, if we're making the right investments in people's lives over time, those results will come about. Remember the story of my wife I shared back in chapter 7? She encountered believers who poured themselves into her life, some of whom

> We need to embrace a long-term view of what we do, knowing that today's seed-sowing will only be fully understood in the light of eternity."

she doesn't even know their names, but their investment in her life would have significant life altering positive impacts. She's a teacher now because of a third grade teacher who cried when Heather left that school. Christians from a local church once brought groceries to a drug house that her family was staying in, and one of the ladies from that church made her the best sandwich she had ever had. Years later, she went to a church when she was invited because she remembered that Christians make good sandwiches. The Lord used this to bring her to faith because someone demonstrated Christ-like compassion years before. We need to embrace a long-term view of what we do, knowing that today's seed-sowing will only be fully understood in the light of eternity.

Money. The next characteristic is money. The residents of Middle Classburg view money as something to be managed, while the residents of Povertyville see money as something to be spent. The view of money for Christians is that money is something to be stewarded. All things are the Lords and he has entrusted us to steward some of it. Writing to his young apprentice, Titus, the Apostle Paul says:

"For an overseer, as God's steward, must be above reproach. He must not be arrogant or quick-tempered or a drunkard or violent or greedy for gain, but hospitable, a lover of good, self-controlled, upright, holy, and disciplined. He must hold firm to the trustworthy word as taught, so that he may be able to give instruction in sound doctrine and also to rebuke those who contradict it" (Titus 1:7-9).

Let me offer three key points from this passage. *First*, we don't own the money and things we have; rather, they have been given to us by God to oversee and to steward them well. God owns the stuff. It's not ours, and we did not bring it into the world with us. It will not leave with us when we go. So, if we see everything we have as not our own, but as God's, then we can be open handed with our money and possessions. *Second*, we need to steward the resources God has given us. Stewardship means the careful and responsible management of something entrusted to one's care. As Christians, our calling is to be careful and to responsibly manage the resources entrusted to us. This means we should keep a budget, set priorities that are aligned with God's priorities, and manage the money and resources we have been entrusted accordingly. *Third*, Titus 1:7-9 not only tells us to be stewards of what God has given us to oversee, but it also tells us how we're to live while we're doing it. We must not be arrogant, quick tempered, an alcoholic, an addict, or greedy. Why? Because each of those character issues would cause us to misunderstand and mismanage the money and resources God has entrusted to us. Paul goes on to say that we should be hospitable, love good, and exhibit self-control, while leading an upright, holy, and disciplined life.

In the Kingdom of God, it's not about creating a budget because you tend to make bad decisions with your money. It's about recognizing that what you have doesn't belong to you. It has been given to you for a time to manage in the best way possible. If you really think about it, living out this one verse completely transforms most of the poor individual behaviors that behavior modification programs try (and often fail) to

> In the Kingdom of God, it's not about creating a budget because you tend to make bad decisions with your money.

change. Managing money is relatively easy and subjective. But God desires something more. He wants to bring about a heart-transformation that turns both a spender or a manager into a steward for the Kingdom of God.

Worldview. We discovered earlier in chapter 6 that the Middle Class perspective or Worldview tends to be regional. The residents of Middle Classburg look to see what's happening in their city, in their area, maybe a little bit of what's happening on the state and national level, but not a whole lot globally. For the residents of Povertyville, their worldview tends to be ultra local, right here inside this city, even from this street to that street.

But what about for the Christian? What should our worldview be? It should be global. In fact, some of the last words spoken by the Risen Christ embody a command to go and make disciples of all the nations (Matthew 28:18-20). His last words to his disciples, before being taken up into heaven were, "… and you will be my witnesses in Jerusalem and in all Judea and Samaria, and to the end of the earth" (Acts 1:8).

Let's face it, going "to the end of the earth" sounds very global! That idea may sound intimidating to you and me, but you and I live in an age of global connectivity. We have the internet, Facebook, Twitter, worldwide media channels, satellites, and more to connect us with the world. If taking the good news of God's reconciliation in Christ seems intimidating to you and me, just imagine how that must have sounded to twelve poor dudes from the Middle East who had to walk everywhere they went! Then God says, "Now, you're going to take this good news to all of the nations." That must have seemed crazy-impossible to these guys.

But the amazing thing is they did it! And 2,000 some-odd years later, here we are. However many thousands of miles away from that place where it all began, we're still talking about it! They actually did it, and believers throughout the centuries have been doing this very thing all over the world. That's what it means to have a global worldview that sees and cares about what's happening around the world.

We'll finish this discussion and complete the chart in the next chapter.

Reflecting and Looking Ahead

1. Reflecting on this chapter, what did you discover about how Jesus transforms us and the way we see the world around us?

2. The author made the statement, "Jesus didn't come to make poor people into Middle Class people. Jesus came to make all people God's people." Do you agree or disagree? Explain.

3. How has your citizenship in the Kingdom of God changed the way you see the world around you?

For Additional Study

For additional individual or group study, including a more in-depth look at what Scripture teaches on this topic, see the Study Guide for this book.

The Ghetto, the Garden and the Gospel

12
Contentment In Love

"Not that I am speaking of being in need, for I have learned in whatever situation I am to be content." (Philippians 4:11)

In the previous chapter, we looked at how the values of the Kingdom of God transform our understanding of *Time, Money* and our *Worldview*. Now, we want to look at how those values transform our *Emphasis*, our *Driving Force* and our *Mental Model*. Let's finish filling in our "Understanding Our Differences" table.

Emphasis. As we discussed at length in chapter 6, the Emphasis in Middle Classburg, America, is on quality. We go to a restaurant, we order our food, and we take the first bite. That's when our server shows up and asks, as we're chewing that first bite, "How's it taste?" At that moment, the emphasis is on quality. But in Povertyville, USA, things are a little different. When we're invited to a home in Povertyville, we're given food, and as we're almost done, our host asks us, "Did you get enough?" Now, the emphasis is on quantity, rather than quality. Often, they'll proceed to serve you more!

This even becomes a cultural thing. I was in Greece when I made a major social faux pas. I didn't leave any food on the plate. I came from a household where we were expected to clean our plate. Greek food is amazing, so I ate and enjoyed every bite. But in Greece you're expected to leave a little bit on your plate. It's like saying to your host, "Thank you, I had enough. You gave me more than enough to eat." Failing to do so is seen as an insult to the host. They even have a name for this food left on the plate: they call it *"God's portion."* Some Greeks will actually separate that part out and leave it on the edge of the plate before they even start eating, as a sign of respect and a way of saying, "Yes, I've had enough, thank you."

Okay, if the residents of Middle Classburg ask, "How's it taste?", and if their cousins in Povertyville ask "Did you get enough?", what question should Christians be asking? "Are you content with what you have?" For the Christian, the emphasis should be on Contentment and whether or not we are grateful for what God has provided. Paul talks about contentment in his letter to the believers in Philippi when he says:

The Ghetto, the Garden and the Gospel

"Not that I am speaking of being in need, for I have learned in whatever situation I am to be content. I know how to be brought low, and I know how to abound. In any and every circumstance, I have learned the secret of facing plenty and hunger, abundance and need. I can do all things through him who strengthens me." (Philippians 4:11-13)

For this to make sense, we need to take a moment and define contentment. The New Testament idea of contentment is built on a Greek word meaning "to be or to have enough" (Luke 3:14, 1 Timothy 6:8, and Hebrews 13:5).33 Paul uses the noun form of this word in Philippians 4:10 (and again in 1 Timothy 6:6). A school of Greek philosophers, known as the Stoics, had built a philosophy of self-denial around this word. For the Stoic, contentment was a human achievement of the will based on radical self-denial. But for the Christian, contentment is different. The Apostle understood contentment as complete Christ-dependence, believing that whatever God supplies is enough for the need at that moment. That's why Paul could say in complete faith, "But if we have food and clothing, with these we will be content" (1 Timothy 6:8). As Christians, contentment is not an achievement of the will, but a spiritual work of faith by the Holy Spirit as we trust God to be enough, whatever our situation might be.

> For the Christian, the emphasis should be on contentment and whether or not we are grateful for what God has provided.

The sign of genuine contentment in the life of the believer is that we're at peace with what God is doing in our lives at the moment. How is this kind of contentment even possible? Paul tells us in verse 13 at the end of this passage, "I can do all things through him who strengthens me." It's a verse Christians frequently use in a context of achievement, or of overcoming some challenge or obstacle. But the true context, as it's used here, has to do with being content with whatever we have, regardless of our economic situation. This kind of genuine contentment is a work of the

> The sign of genuine contentment in the life of the believer is that we're at peace with what God is doing in our lives at the moment.

Holy Spirit in our lives.

Let's face it. This is about as counter-cultural as we could possibly get in the United States. There is nothing in our culture that tells us we should be content. Just the opposite! Commercial advertising is designed to generate massive discontentment, convincing us that our lives are incomplete without that new car, the newest smartphone, the latest designer clothes, those expensive athletic shoes, or the slim waistline. Commercials literally sing the glories of buying things while happy, smiling people dance around their living room, celebrating their latest purchases while not-so-subtly inviting us to "come, join us." Can you imagine a Fortune 500 Company spending $5 million for a 30-second Super Bowl commercial, just to tell you to be content with what you already have?! No, me neither.

But, as believers, genuine contentment is our calling. Whatever our economic condition, God has provided for us, and He will continue to provide. We are called to be content and grateful for what He has given us. This idea that inner contentment is something we should

> The scales of the Kingdom measure the things of our lives very differently.

strive for may be a very counter-cultural idea, but it's also very biblical. These are the inverted values of the Kingdom of God. The scales of the Kingdom measure the things of our lives very differently. On one arm of God's scale is the pearl of great value (Matthew 13:46), while the other arm of the scale holds everything else in our lives. And we're called to choose.

Driving Force. Earlier we discovered that the Driving Force for the residents of Middle Classburg, America, tends to be achievement. For the residents of Povertyville, their driving force tends to be relationships. After all, those relationships enable you to survive in Povertyville. But for the believer, our driving force is love. Specifically, love for God and love for your neighbor. Jesus spells this out for us very clearly in Matthew 22:35-40. In the lead-up to this passage, the religious leaders make several futile attempts to trap Jesus with answers to trick questions. Finally, a lawyer (an expert in the Old Testament Law) steps forward with another question:

The Ghetto, the Garden and the Gospel

"And one of them, a lawyer, asked him a question to test him. 'Teacher, which is the great commandment in the Law?' And he said to him,'You shall love the Lord your God with all your heart and with all your soul and with all your mind. This is the great and first commandment. And a second is like it: You shall love your neighbor as yourself. On these two commandments depend all the Law and the Prophets'." (Matthew 22:35-40)

There is, perhaps, no greater single summary of biblical truth than this one from the lips of Jesus. The driving force of our calling is to love God completely and to love our neighbor sacrificially. The Fall into sin, which resulted in us being evicted from the Garden and being cast into the Ghetto, broke these two relationships. Sin broke both our vertical relationship with God and our horizontal relationship with one another. God's redemption and reconciliation in Christ restores both broken relationships. We now have the ability to love God completely and to love our neighbor sacrificially.

The Apostle John reinforces these thoughts on our horizontal and vertical relationships when he says:

"We love because he first loved us. If anyone says, 'I love God,' and hates his brother, he is a liar; for he who does not love his brother whom he has seen cannot love God whom he has not seen. And this commandment we have from him: whoever loves God must also love his brother." (1 John 4:19-21)

We can now love God completely because He first loved us and restored our vertical relationship with Him in Christ. But He has also restored our horizontal relationships with others, giving us a ministry of spreading reconciliation and enabling us to genuinely and sacrificially love our neighbors.

Mental Model. As we discovered earlier, the residents of Middle Classburg, America, have a mental model best described as pizza slices, where the slices don't touch each other. Each slice has its own ingredients, and we don't like the slices to touch or interact. This creates a highly segmented view of life. But in Povertyville, the mental model is a little different. It's a ball of yarn where everything touches, everything is intertwined and interconnected. As Christians, our Mental Model is very different. It's a cross. Why? Because the cross is the ultimate picture of profound sacrificial love -- a giving up of our own wants and desires, and a laying down of our own preferences, in order to

> The cross is the ultimate picture of profound sacrificial love.

serve others and to seek their reconciliation. It's what Jesus did for us, and it's what we're called to do for others.

This model of self-sacrifice has played out in many different ways throughout church history. For example, the fact that you and I have a Bible today that we can read for ourselves in our own language is the result of believers who sacrificed their lives to bring us that Bible. If you and I really thought about how many people were murdered just so that we could have this book, we might take it a little bit more seriously and read it with quite a bit more intensity. Imagine if someone handed you a love letter and told you hundreds of thousands of people died so that you could read this letter. I would imagine you would take it with trembling hands and read it thoughtfully and completely. However, since it is on our phone, on our computer, and is so easily accessible to us we tend to not think of it as highly as we should. The Bible we hold in our hands today represents the tangible result of sacrificial love.

Another example of sacrificial love on a smaller scale might involve sacrificing our personal preferences. This is a hard one for churches. Christian author and activist Jim Wallis started his career negotiating treaties between rival gangs in Los Angeles. He worked with the Crips and the Bloods in L.A., to negotiate a treaty between the two gangs. Eventually, Jim moved from working with inner-city gangs to working on issues involving church unity. Jim confessed that it was easier to get inner-city gangs to work together than to get churches to work together. Ouch. As Christians, we're called to sacrificial love, and sometimes that means we're called to sacrifice our preferences for the sake of others.

Several years ago, I was part of a church re-plant or re-boot of an older church where a young pastor had come in and had begun to change things -- the environment, the music, and much more. One of the leading elders during that time confessed that he hated the new music, but he would always say this: "I hate the music, it's too loud and it's not the hymns I grew up with, but as long as people are being saved I can lay down my preferences for them." That's a practical expression of sacrificial love.

You and I hear stories about church fights over such things as the color of the carpet, over the new drapes, over changing out the pews to chairs, or over replacing (or removing) the hymnals. Ultimately, these are all peripheral things and are all things that are not actually essential. We need to focus on what is actually essential. And part of that essential focus may be laying down our own preferences for the sake of others. Maybe it means that, to engage a particular neighborhood, you'll need to lay down some preferences about language for the sake of that large portion of the community that speaks Spanish or getting a little bit outside of our comfort zone on our worship styles.

At that same church I mentioned, we had an intern who was an African-American man. One Sunday, he was standing in the back of the church when he turned to me and said, "You keep playing the same song." I was surprised. "No, they're all different songs," I insisted. What he meant was, as an African-American man, all the worship songs sounded like the same Hillsong-kind-of-approach to music. He wanted me to understand that there are many different worship styles and many different cultural aspects to worship. Maybe, if we laid down our particular preference a little and incorporated some of those other worship styles, it might be good. So we tried a musical diversity month, where each Sunday we played a different musical style. One Sunday we had gospel, one Sunday was Country, we even had a liturgical Sunday. When it was all said and done we ended up incorporating elements of many different styles into our worship services moving forward. Our congregation surged as hundreds of Black college students began attending. Laying down our preferences and allowing people to worship in a way that resonates with them and that they enjoy is a form of sacrificial love and service on our part.

The complete Understanding or Differences chart below is the culmination of all of the things we have discussed to this point. One earlier reviewer of this book called it the "Golden Chart" and said the chart below is worth more than any price we could charge for this book. Take some time to examine the chart and think about where you fall in each of these areas. What areas do you fall short of the Christian categories and default towards one of the other categories? What can you do to change that?

Understanding Our Differences			
Characteristic	Middle Class	Poverty	Christian
Time	Future	Present/Now	Eternal
Money	Manage/Save	Spend	Steward
Worldview	City/Region	Ultra Local	Global
Emphasis	Quality	Quantity	Contentment
Driving Force	Achievement	Relationships	Love
Mental Model	Segmented Pizza	Ball of Yarn	The Cross

A Definition and a Challenge

Earlier, in chapter 5, we defined Middle Class as that point at which you have sufficient resources for a stable environment today and are investing extra resources in a stable tomorrow. We also defined Poverty as that point at which you lack the daily resources needed to maintain a stable environment today. What we haven't done yet, and what we need to do to finish our "Understanding Our Differences" chart, is to define what we mean when we say Christian. At the risk of provoking a food fight at the next church potluck, I want us to define Christian this way:

> *A Christian is a person who has come to the point at which one is so affected by the love of God, through the good news of Jesus Christ, that he or she is constrained to make the will of Christ the will of his or her heart and life.*

In the Kingdom of God, our faith and discipleship represent the point at which we no longer have a choice. It's the point where we say, "Alright God, because you love me and you've forgiven me and reconciled me, I'm laying everything down. Do with me what you will."

I have a friend who is probably the most devoted kind of "crazy missionary" I know. He's one of those people who lives his life with his hair on fire for God. He's a guy who just lays it all down for Jesus. When war started in Tunisia and began the Arab Spring, he was on a plane headed there a day later. Why? Because people are in need. His attitude is simple, "I'm going to lay it all down for Jesus." What's more, he has a wife and three little kids. Now, I'm a missions guy and I'm thinking, *This is scary. We don't know what's really happening there. We don't know what it's going to be like when you hit the ground. And there's a real possibility you might not come back alive.* His response? "I'm compelled to go, regardless of what happens."

Let's be real. That's a scarier way to live life. It's definitely not the response of most of us Christians living in Middle Classburg, America. But it's also a freer way to live. And it confronts us with a discipleship question: As Christians and as disciples of the Kingdom, are we living out the life that God has called us to? Too many of us are walking in a fear that God has not called us to. I am not talking about being as extreme as going into a war zone. Rather, we fear engaging with our neighbors. We fear actually going out and walking around our neighborhood and talking to people who may not be like us. Fear of getting to know them for who they are. As Christians, as committed disciples of the Kingdom, and as Ambassadors of Christ, our calling is to lay down our preferences and our fears for the sake of the gospel. It's a small price to pay to fully lay hold of the pearl of great value. As Jim Elliott so passionately wrote as he reflected on his calling to a life of missions and sacrificial service, *He is no fool who gives what he cannot keep to gain that which he cannot lose.*

Reflecting And Looking Ahead

1. Reflecting on this chapter and the previous chapter, what have you discovered about the transformed thinking of new creations toward the world around us that you didn't understand before?

2. How is the Christian view of contentment as Christ-dependence different from the Stoic view of contentment as radical self-denial.

3. Reflect on this principle from chapter 12, "For the Christian, the emphasis should be on contentment, and whether or not I'm grateful for what God has provided." Do you agree or disagree? Explain. What do you think is the biblical relationship between gratitude and contentment?

For Additional Study

For additional individual or group study, including a more in-depth look at what Scripture teaches on this topic, see the Study Guide for this book.

The Ghetto, the Garden and the Gospel

13
Seek the Welfare of the City

"But seek the welfare of the city where I have sent you into exile, and pray to the LORD on its behalf, for in its welfare you will find your welfare." (Jeremiah 29:7)

Earlier, in chapter 11, we spent some time looking at 2 Corinthians 5:17 and talking about old things passing away and new things coming. In our context of understanding poverty, this means that our old Middle Classburg or Povertyville ways of thinking and categorizing need to pass away and be replaced with a more biblical way of thinking about these issues. It's time to think transformed thoughts about the city and the people you and I have been called to serve.

Seek the Welfare of the City

Writing to Christian believers in the Greek city of Corinth, Paul reminds them that as new creations, they also have a new ministry, "All this is from God, who through Christ reconciled us to himself and gave us the ministry of reconciliation" (2 Corinthians 5:18). God has given us a ministry of reconciliation. But what does that mean? What does it mean to work for reconciliation?

To help us think this through, let's look at a familiar passage from the Old Testament book of Jeremiah. "But seek the welfare of the city where I have sent you into exile, and pray to the LORD on its behalf, for in its welfare you will find your welfare" (Jeremiah 29:7). In 586 B.C. the Babylonians conquered the Southern Kingdom of Judah, captured the city of Jerusalem, and took most of the inhabitants to Babylon as captives. The question on everyone's mind in Babylon was, "What are we supposed to do here?" Through the prophet Jeremiah, God spoke and called His people to seek the welfare of the city where they had been taken into captivity because in its welfare they will find their own welfare.

Could you imagine the frustration and anger they must have felt to hear these words? They have been through war, their friends and family members have been killed, their homes destroyed, they are now taken captive in a foreign land and God is telling them to seek to better Babylon.

The Ghetto, the Garden and the Gospel

Isn't that a strange thing for God to say to His people? It's no wonder Jeremiah got beat up so much, and that most of the prophets got beaten and killed. But isn't the message of Jeremiah very similar to what Jesus told the disciples when He said, "Love your enemies and pray for those who persecute you" (Matthew 5:44)? For Jeremiah and the Israelites, the enemies were Babylonian; for Jesus and the disciples, the enemies were Roman. But the instructions were the same. The New Testament describes believers as exiles and sojourners (1 Peter 1:1; 2:11) -- people called to live in a place that is not their home. Like those exiles of Jeremiah's day, Scripture calls us to seek the welfare of the city where we live because in its welfare we will find our own welfare.

> Seek the welfare of the City where you live because in its welfare you will find your welfare.

Let's face it. Christians in America are typically not seen as seeking the welfare of their cities. We create large church buildings outside of the most needy communities. We send our kids to private schools instead of investing in public schools. We rail against the possibility of low income apartments or homes being built near our homes. We try to set up our homes like our own little kingdoms insulated from the problems of the community around us. However, scripture says that this place is not our home. We have been sent here as Ambassadors to seek the welfare of this place.

The Hebrew word *shalom*, translated *welfare* in Jeremiah 29:7, embodies a sense of health, wholeness, and peace that no single English word can capture, so we use words like *welfare*. But the message communicated by shalom, and by God's command for us to seek it, is profound. If we want *shalom* for ourselves, we have to seek it for others. If we want peace, health, wholeness, and welfare for ourselves and our families, then we have to be willing to seek it for others and their families. And if the residents of Middle Classburg, America, want shalom for themselves, then they have to be willing to seek it for the residents of Povertyville, USA, too.

> Regardless of where we live, our personal welfare is tied to the welfare of others.

130

Why Are You Fasting and Praying?

There's another passage I want us to look at that speaks to these issues. It's from the prophet Isaiah, who ministered some 700 years before Christ. I have a fondness for Isaiah because, when I read Isaiah, his words sound so much like the words of Jesus. If you didn't know the context (that it's Isaiah), you would almost think that it was Jesus saying these things although they were spoken 700 years prior to Christ's ministry on earth. The particular passage I want us to consider is found in Isaiah 58:

> "Is not this the fast that I choose: to loose the bonds of wickedness, to undo the straps of the yoke, to let the oppressed go free, and to break every yoke? Is it not to share your bread with the hungry and bring the homeless poor into your house; when you see the naked, to cover him, and not to hide yourself from your own flesh?" (Isaiah 58:6-7).

Two things stand out to me about this passage. *First,* I can't help but notice how much this sounds like Jesus' sermon we discussed earlier where he says he will know us by how we serve the least of these. That same one that discusses the eternal consequences of not serving the least of these. *Second,* it confronts us with the true purpose of an important spiritual discipline: fasting.

How many of us have ever done a fast, intentionally abstaining from food or something else for an extended period of time? If you have, did you think about why you were doing it? Did you think, "I'm doing this because I want to serve somebody else?" Or did you think, I'm fasting to hear what God is calling me to do, or to know God's will, or to ask God to help me solve a problem in my life? Usually, when we fast, we're praying about something for ourselves. But here in Isaiah 58, God is talking about fasting and praying for others -- doing without for ourselves so that we can serve others. That's a different way of approaching prayer and fasting, isn't it? The most clear example of this type of fasting in the modern era was not seen from a Christian, but from the Hindu man Mahatma Gandhi. He fasted for different causes: against violent protest actions of radical factions of the independence movement, in support of the "untouchables" and in opposition to the British constitutional proposal based on the separation of castes, for Hindu-Muslim unity, against communal riots. In all of these fasts, they were never done for himself. Could you imagine that you could stop a war by fasting? Such was the admiration for this man that, that is what happened. So, here is my question: If scripture talks about this type of fasting for Christians, then why don't we see it or hear about it more? When was the last time we as Christians in Middle Classburg, America, spent time fasting and praying for our cousins living in Povertyville, USA?

The reality is that living life in this way and fasting in this way come with real inherent risks to ourselves. Are you ready to "bring the homeless poor into your house"? How many of us are ready to drive to "that part of town," search under the bridge and say to a homeless person, "You're coming to my house to stay." That causes fear and tension for most of us, doesn't it? As I've mentioned a couple of times in this book, I run a homeless shelter. And, yes, I have brought someone who was homeless home to live with us. This particular time turned into an amazing experience. I have helped thousands of homeless in my life, but have only brought one into my home. The reason this one time was different was because I felt the Holy Spirit leading me in this direction. However, I invited my wife to meet this particular young woman and while we were having lunch with her my wife leaned over and said, "I think we should invite her to live with us." We both were compelled by the Spirit to act. So know that I am not saying to take every person on the street into your home, but I am saying get to know those experiencing homelessness and be open to the Spirit's leading for how that relationship can develop. If we never get out and build relationships with the "least of these," we'll never get to the point of doing what Isaiah is talking about here.

Isaiah goes on to say in verse 12 that if we do these things, "Your ancient ruins shall be rebuilt; you shall raise up the foundations of many generations; you shall be called the repairer of the breach, the restorer of streets to dwell in." According to Isaiah, we're supposed to be repairers of the breach and restorers of streets to dwell in. Doesn't that sound a little like the work of reconciliation? Yes, it does! This is how you and I are supposed to bring about the ministry of reconciliation that God has given us. We're supposed to engage our communities, to fast and pray for their shalom, and to sacrifice ourselves and our preferences for the sake of others. That's when we will actually begin to reconcile and restore some of this brokenness in our neighborhoods, our communities, our cities, and our culture. This is how our broken relationship with others begins to be renewed, and how our relationship with creation is repaired.

Reflecting and Looking Ahead

1. Reflecting on this chapter, what new thing did you learn about what it means to "seek the welfare of the city" that you did not understand before?

2. Scripture is clear that God has given us a ministry of reconciliation. Discuss some practical steps you, your church, or your ministry could take, and issues you could address, which would embody working for the reconciliation and "welfare" of your Community.

3. In this chapter, the author said that "regardless of where we live, our personal welfare is tied to the welfare of others." Do you agree or disagree? Why? Explain how your own welfare is tied to the welfare of those around you.

For Additional Study

For additional individual or group study, including a more in-depth look at what Scripture teaches on this topic, see the Study Guide for this book.

The Ghetto, the Garden and the Gospel

14

An Ambassador, Not A Judge

"In Christ, God was reconciling the world to himself, not counting their trespasses against them, and entrusting to us the message of reconciliation. Therefore, we're ambassadors for Christ, God making his appeal through us. We implore you on behalf of Christ, be reconciled to God." (2 Corinthians 5:19-20)

Avoiding Judgmental Attitudes

As we complete our thoughts on 2 Corinthians 5:17-21 and what it means to be ministers of reconciliation, I want us to reflect on two big ideas. The first big idea has to do with what it means to judge (or not judge) others. In verse 19, the Apostle Paul says that in Christ, "God was reconciling the world to himself, not counting their trespasses against them." In His work to reconcile us with Himself, God didn't count our trespasses against us. In our work of reconciliation among the broken people and places of our communities, the same principle needs to apply. How do we count people's trespasses against them? By our judgmental attitudes toward others.

I really can't emphasize this enough. People living in generational poverty are experts at reading our non-verbals, and our non-verbals frequently reek of judgment. These folks come from unsafe environments, and they have to be able to "read the room" to understand if you're a danger or not. As a result, they are able to read your non-verbals, which means they can tell if you're being judgmental, whether you say it or not. They're going to read you and ask themselves, "Is this person judging me?" This is the number one complaint I heard from people in need when I ran a food pantry and clothing ministry in Texas, "Your volunteers treated me with disrespect. They judged me before they knew me. They judged me coming into this place." As a result, this is one of the core values we emphasize at the shelter I oversee; to be non-judgmental toward the people we work with. We talk about it amongst each other, and we encourage the guests to talk about it among themselves.

Jesus On Judging

Jesus talked about this issue of judging others when He told the disciples:

The Ghetto, the Garden and the Gospel

"Judge not, that you be not judged. For with the judgment you pronounce you will be judged, and with the measure you use it will be measured to you. Why do you see the speck that is in your brother's eye, but don't notice the log that is in your own eye? Or how can you say to your brother, 'Let me take the speck out of your eye,' when there is the log in your own eye? You hypocrite, first take the log out of your own eye, and then you will see clearly to take the speck out of your brother's eye." (Matthew 7:1-5)

Jesus uses two metaphors to describe the hypocrisy of judging others. The first is the image of seeing a wood chip in someone else's eye while ignoring the tree-log in our own (other people's trespasses always look bigger than our own). The second metaphor, which

> Hypocrisy is using one standard with others and a different standard for yourself.

often gets overlooked, is the image of a measuring cup: "with the measure you use it will be measured to you." In the metaphor of a measuring cup, Jesus defines a hypocrite as someone with two different measuring cups for measuring out God's grace -- one measuring cup to measure out God's grace for themselves, but a different (smaller) measuring cup to measure out God's grace for everyone else. Hypocrisy is using one standard with others and a different standard for yourself. God is not stingy with his grace towards us and we, therefore, should not be stingy with grace towards others.

Judging others means we have chosen to focus on someone else's issues (i.e., their trespasses) while ignoring our own very real issues. That's the type of hypocrisy that Jesus

> Our calling is to work for their reconciliation.

warned against in Matthew 7. It's asking God for more grace for ourselves than we're willing to give to others. The cure to a judgmental spirit is to realize that we all have issues, but that Christ came to reconcile all of us, not counting our trespasses against us. Therefore, we have no right before God to judge others for their issues. Our calling is to work for their reconciliation. Which means we must lay down our judgment, try to understand, and then share good news. What a beautiful message it is that although all of us are guilty and have fallen short of the glory of God, he has freedom for us, not condemnation. This is the message that you take to those in need; and those in need of hearing it include you, me and everyone else on this planet. That is good news. That's the gospel.

What it Means to Be an Ambassador

The second big idea to think about is found in 2 Corinthians 5:20, where Paul declares that we're called to be "ambassadors for Christ." I love that word, ambassadors. Let's start with a definition. According to Merriam-Webster, an ambassador is "a diplomatic agent of the highest rank accredited to a foreign government or sovereign as the resident representative of his or her own government or sovereign or appointed for a special and often temporary diplomatic assignment." Think about that. In the Kingdom of our sovereign God, you and I are "diplomatic agents of the highest rank." On a practical level, ambassadors have very important and specific tasks. An ambassador is:

- Someone who represents one Kingdom in a foreign land
- Someone who works for peace and makes treaties
- Someone who promotes understanding between their home culture and the new culture;
- Someone who builds trust between cultures and people
- Someone who has or speaks with the authority of the One who sent him or her
- Someone who knows where they live is not their home, it is a temporary assignment

As Christians and ambassadors, we are all these things. We are representatives of Christ and His Kingdom to people who don't know Him. We are here to proclaim peace between God and those for whom Christ died to reconcile. Our task is to promote better understanding between the Kingdom of God and the culture where we find ourselves. We're bridge-builders between the Kingdom of God and those around us. We speak with the authority of the King. Our task is to promote better understanding

> Our task is to promote better understanding between the Kingdom of God and the culture where we find ourselves.

between the Kingdom of God and the culture where we find ourselves. Lastly, we realize that this is a temporary assignment before we return home.

"We implore you on behalf of Christ, be reconciled to God. For our sake he made him to be sin who knew no sin, so that in him we might become the righteousness of God" (2 Corinthians 5:20-21). This is the message that you and I are supposed to bring. It's the same message that the Apostle Paul proclaimed on his worldwide tour of Roman prisons. But, oftentimes, you and I are fearful of being ambassadors and proclaiming the message we've been given because we think someone might be offended, or they might look at us weird. But, as disciples of the Kingdom, God often uses our obedience -- what others see as "weird" -- in ways we could never anticipate. And that deserves a story.

When I was at Baylor University, I dated the daughter of a United States diplomat. Her father was stationed in Germany while we dated. One year her mother had this really crazy idea. Well every country has their national day of celebration, like our Fourth of July. The US diplomats and most diplomats attend the parties for the national days of the most prominent countries, USA, England, Germany, France, China, Russia, etc. However, one year my girlfriend's mother said, This year I want to go and celebrate all the 'stans.' The 'stans' were countries like Afghanistan, Turkmenistan, Uzbekistan, Tajikistan, Pakistan, etc. This was very out of the ordinary, but they attended those countries' national day celebrations at those countries' embassies in Germany. In doing so, they began meeting all of these people from these often neglected countries.

Then, something unexpected happened. The attacks of 9/11 happened and shortly afterwards the United States went to war with Afghanistan. In order to do this the US would have to fly over and even land planes in countries that surround Afghanistan. In order to do that they would need to negotiate treaties with those countries. So the State Department began looking for diplomats who had relationships with these "stan" countries. As it turns out my girlfriend's father in Germany was the person in the State Department who had built relationships with the "stan" countries. As a result, he was able to negotiate treaties for the U.S. to operate throughout that part of the world. And it all came from what everyone thought was just a crazy idea.

I tell this story to make a point. Some of the relationships that you start to build now are going to have future ramifications that you and I can't predict or anticipate today. You and I simply don't know where those relationships will come into play in your future or the future of your ministry. The time may come when you will need to call on someone you've been loving and serving, and they will be able to help you with a need that only they can meet. In the words of Mordecai to Esther, "And who knows whether you have not come to the kingdom for such a time as this?"(Esther 4:14).

Thoughts on Serving from Our Gifts

When it comes to ministry and sacrificial service, people frequently do not believe God can use them because they are not as gifted as someone else. However, what we find in scripture is God looking for people with willing hearts, he will then use both their gifts and their weaknesses for His glory. God called Moses and when Moses's heart was right and he was willing God used him to be His spokesman to lead the Israelites out of bondage, even though Moses had a major speech impediment. Moses was a called and gifted leader whom God used in incredible ways. But God also partnered Moses with Aaron, who became Moses' mouthpiece.

A different biblical example is Joseph, and this one is really more to our point. Joseph was an incredibly gifted prophet and seer. God gave him profound visions concerning his own future, which Joseph shared until he had irritated almost everybody. While Joseph was very gifted, he was also young, brash, and immature. Joseph had character flaws which threatened to overshadow his calling and his gifts.

> Left to ourselves, you and I tend to destroy with our character what we build with our gift.

There is an important ministry principle here that we need to wrap our heads around. Left to ourselves, you and I tend to destroy with our character what we build with our gift.

God had gifted Joseph with prophetic insight to see the future, to interpret dreams, and to implement wise strategies. His gifting was profound. God knew

139

that one day Joseph would rise to great power and prominence, would rule over Egypt, and would save his people. But God also knew that Joseph's personal character flaws had to be addressed or they would prevent Joseph from achieving everything God had for him. In the providence of God, Joseph would spend the next fifteen years in captivity, where he would learn personal humility, trust for God, and service to others, while having his character tested and refined. But the day would come when Pharaoh would be able to say with confidence:

"'Can we find a man like this, in whom is the Spirit of God?' Then Pharaoh said to Joseph, 'Since God has shown you all this, there is none so discerning and wise as you are. You shall be over my house, and all my people shall order themselves as you command. Only as regards the throne will I be greater than you.' And Pharaoh said to Joseph, 'See, I have set you over all the land of Egypt'." (Genesis 41:38-41)

Scripture is clear that God has given each of us a gift which He expects us to use to further His Kingdom purposes:

"As each has received a gift, use it to serve one another, as good stewards of God's varied grace: whoever speaks, as one who speaks oracles of God; whoever serves, as one who serves by the strength that God supplies—in order that in everything God may be glorified through Jesus Christ. To him belong glory and dominion forever and ever. Amen." (1 Peter 4:10-11)

The purpose of your gift is to serve others and to glorify God. To not use the gift He has given you is to ignore the clear teaching of Scripture, and to fail to bring glory to God. But as we use our gift to sacrificially serve others, remember this: God is as concerned with your character as He is with your gift. Don't be surprised if He calls you to ministry situations which not only utilize your gift, but which challenge your character and stretch your weakness to the point of making you teachable. That's what He did for Joseph. And that's how Christ-likeness gets formed in us.

Reflecting And Looking Ahead

1. Reflecting on this chapter, what did you learn about the difference between being a judge toward the people around us and being an Ambassador for the Kingdom of God?

2. In our work of reconciliation, seeking the welfare of the city, and reaching out to serve the poor and marginalized of our community, what are some of the ways we sometimes act as judges rather than as Ambassadors of the Kingdom?

3. In chapter 14, the author made this statement, "A hypocrite is someone who uses one measuring cup to measure out God's grace for themselves, but uses a different (smaller) measuring cup to measure out God's grace for everyone else. Hypocrisy is treating others differently than we treat ourselves; it's being 'stingy' with God's grace toward others and their issues." Do you agree or disagree? Explain.

For Additional Study

For additional individual or group study, including a more in-depth look at what Scripture teaches on this topic, see the Study Guide for this book.

The Ghetto, the Garden and the Gospel

15
The Iron Rule

"So whatever you wish that others would do to you, do also to them, for this is the Law and the Prophets." (Matthew 7:12)

A Missions Assessment

Now, it's time for us to do a missions/ministry assessment. And we're going to do it at the Mayukwayukwa Refugee Settlement, established in Zambia in 1966 to host refugees fleeing Angola's civil war. In the picture below, volunteers are passing out food. There's some type of food distribution going on in the refugee camp. Are these people doing something good? Your initial response is probably, "Sure. They appear to be caring for people's needs."

Let me give you a little more context of this picture. This refugee settlement was one of the first United Nation refugee settlements ever set up (back in 1966), and it's still home to over 11,000 refugees today. That's fifty-eight years, as of the writing of this book, that people in this camp have been living dependent on food assistance for their daily survival. Multiple generations have now been born, raised, and had children of their own in this camp. So here is my question, are they doing the right thing for these people? The answer is, "No." These people are not equipped to be self-sufficient. They are not being provided with opportunities or training necessary for a better life beyond being dependent for their survival. In fact, this is the refugee settlement that requests the most food assistance each year. The man handing out the food is forty years old, and he's lived his entire life in this refugee settlement. He's Angolan by ethnicity but has never been to Angola. His whole life has been spent in this refugee settlement in Zambia. These people should have been resettled into a place where they could thrive.

You would think that someone should have figured out how to resettle 11,000 people in fifty-eight years and equipped them with whatever training and resources they needed to move on. Before you judge this situation too harshly, though, it is important to realize that we, as the modern church, often do the same thing. This is one of the biggest conflicts and challenges we face doing church missions. We attack every situation like it's an emergency. We come in with intervention. We enter every ministry situation with the same approach that we use for a hurricane. A hurricane is a completely different event. It's catastrophic and needs immediate emergency support. However, that emergency support should be brief and limited to a time of crisis. There are a lot of ministries run by Christians for decades, even generations, that only do emergency types of assistance on an everyday basis. When emergency interventions are used as the sole source of support, it can have a harmful effect on the people the ministry is trying to serve by creating in them an unhealthy dependency, rather than building up the person and preparing them to be self-sufficient.

The Iron Rule

Most of us are familiar with The Golden Rule (based on Matthew 7:12) which says, "Do unto others as you would have them do unto you." It means that we treat others the way we would want to be treated. It's a good rule and

> "Don't do something for someone that they can do for themselves."

an important biblical principle that we need more of in our world today. But when we're working with broken and marginalized people, there's another important rule. Author Robert Linthicum lays out what he calls "The Iron Rule," which says, "Don't do something for someone that they can do for themselves."[40]

For my shelter staff and social workers, this is an important working principle. You and I (and almost every social worker I know) have a tendency to say, "Let me do that for you." It's our way of being compassionate and helpful. But what we may be doing is stripping away empowering assets from the people we're serving. "I'll fill out that form for you. I'll do this for you. I'll make that phone call for you." We want to help, but it may not actually be helping that person. It would be better to say, "Here's the number, you can make the call. Do you have a phone that you can use to make the call?" If they don't have a phone, then we can loan them a phone so they can make the call. We can and should assist, but we should not do for someone, because in doing so we are stripping away the very sense of achievement that people need to heal, grow and thrive. Your pity is a poor substitute for someone else's gritty success.

Do you see the difference between that approach and me simply making the call for them? One approach reinforces their inferiority complex, while the other approach says, "You have the power to do this on your own." Our role is to discover the things someone doesn't have the ability to do, and then find ways to empower them to do those. Our role is to be their training wheels, not their bicycle. We're working towards the day when they no longer need us.

When Ministry Is like Family

On a personal level, this has helped me tremendously in parenting, and I'm still working on it daily. My kids come to me with things like, "Dad, can you make me a sandwich." Rather than saying, "Yeah, sure, I can do that," I'm learning to say, "No, you can make a sandwich. Go make your own sandwich." It's not that I want to be a mean dad, and honestly I give in too much, but I need to see this as an empowering moment. What I'm telling them is, "You need to be able to make your own food because that's what adults do. I'm not raising you to be a child. I'm raising you to be an adult." Do you see the difference? Family, ministry, and social work are similar in that we are trying to build people who can feed themselves.

In both ministry and social work we have a tendency to say, "I'll do that for you." We also have a tendency to think, "If I don't do it, the other person is going to do it wrong." Well, maybe that will happen. But what often happens is that we create systems which rely on someone else doing the work for the person in need. We write an application so that only an experienced case manager can fill it out, rather than writing it so that the person who actually needs the assistance can fill it out for themselves. As a result, the person needing assistance has to schedule and wait for an appointment to fill out a form. I know dozens and dozens of non-profit organizations that have hundreds of paid staff members, simply to fill out forms for clients. This is a massive waste of resources in every community in the country. Sure there are some people that need the assistance to fill out a form and those people should receive it, for everyone else the forms should be so simple and easily accessible that they can fill them out themselves. Often, it's because we use wording and terminology that they don't understand. Great. What if we rewrote the application and changed the wording to something a non-professional could understand and complete? How hard is that? But, you wouldn't believe how complex an idea that actually is when you try to get it implemented on the ground.

One clear example of this happened during the COVID19 pandemic. At that time, schools, businesses and just about everything else closed down, except for essential services. This meant that no one

> It seems that The Iron Rule is as hard to get people to obey as The Golden Rule

was getting paid, but rent was still due. So millions of people across the country were late on rent. So the federal government and state governments granted funds to local organizations across the country to help prevent evictions. In our community several organizations received grants to distribute these funds, including mine, Family Promise of Spokane. It was obvious to us that the need was so large that we would need a digital system for processing applications and a way for people to apply from their smartphones. So we built a system to do just that. When we offered it to other organizations, we received all kinds of pushback, including from local by-and-for organizations who told us, "people of color are going to want to come in and meet with someone that looks like them. They are not going to want to do this online." Well over the next two years we would distribute more than $6.2 Million in rental assistance to families. 43% of the applicants that came through the online portal were people of color, which is telling because people of color represent less than 23% of the population of our community. So, as it turns out people in need would rather use their smartphone to apply for help rather than schedule an appointment, find transportation, find someone to watch their kids, gather all the information needed, just to make an appointment. It seems obvious that most of us would prefer the convenience, but the nonprofit world is plagued with organizations that think their staff are the only people qualified to do simple things like fill out forms.

It seems that The Iron Rule is as hard to get people to obey as The Golden

Rule. However, the lesson of The Iron Rule forces us to think differently. Eventually, it forces us to think about going further upriver.

Reflecting and Looking Ahead

1. Reflecting on this chapter, what did the Missions Assessment teach you about missions and ministry that you had not thought about before now?

2. Explain the difference between short-term emergency assistance and equipping people to be self-sufficient long-term, between being someone's training wheels and being their bicycle

3. In Matthew 7:12 Jesus said, "So whatever you wish that others would do to you, do also to them, for this is the Law and the Prophets." That's what we call The Golden Rule. Explain the difference between The Golden Rule and The Iron Rule. How do we keep the two in balance with the compassion of Jesus?

For Additional Study
For additional individual or group study, including a more in-depth look at what Scripture teaches on this topic, see the Study Guide for this book.

16

Going Upriver

"Rescue those who are being taken away to death; hold back those who are stumbling to the slaughter. If you say, 'Behold, we did not know this,' does not he who weighs the heart perceive it? Does not he who keeps watch over your soul know it, and will he not repay man according to his work?" (Proverbs 24:11-12)

There's actually more to this passage than we might think at first. Our first thought might be that it's simply a command to rescue people who are in immediate danger of perishing. It's a command to intervene. That much is true, but there's more. It's also a command to prevent. It's a command to engage in prevention, to "hold back those who are stumbling to the slaughter." This is an important passage to reflect on when we realize that much of our work in ministry and missions tends to fall into three major areas: 1) Intervention, 2) Prevention , and 3) Advancement.

Intervention

When it comes to missions, churches tend to have a significant bias towards intervention. We intervene in difficult situations. We come in and we do things for people. We hand out food and other necessities and do intervention type of work, which is really relief work. And relief work should only be done for a short period of time to stabilize a desperate situation after some disaster like a fire, tornado, hurricane, earthquake or flood. It should not be long-term support. When relief work is done for more than the short term it can end up creating an unhealthy dependency, like the kind we saw in the refugee resettlement camp in the previous chapter.

I once was invited to teach the staff of a non-profit in Texas that had been serving the underprivileged in their community since 1973. It was strange to me that they would need my help, since they had been at this so long. So I asked why they had invited me. Then the director of the non-profit shared with me a story that perfectly illustrates why you should not intervene with relief work longer than is necessary. She shared that she had been sitting in her office when this mom, who was a client of the organization came walking through. The director heard this mom talking to another woman and pointing to staff pictures on the wall. She was telling her, "Oh, this is the person you're going to need to go to for this, and that's the person you're going to need to go to for that." Intrigued by this, the director came out, introduced herself, and said, "So, is this a new client of ours?" To her shock, the woman responded, "No, this is my daughter. I'm just showing her the ropes, because I know that at some point in the future, she's going to need to come here, too." This interaction tormented the Director because what their organization exists to do is provide short term food and clothing relief, not multi-generational dependence.

Are our programs backwards? Are we designing systems so that the next generation will not need our services or are we creating programs that are so short term that they create dependency?

"People in the River" -- An Intervention Parable

What we've described so far in this chapter falls into the area of Intervention. Don't get the wrong idea here. Intervention is good and is often needed. The problem arises when our work of intervention creates long-term dependency, to the point that it becomes generational, as we saw above. So, here's the question that confronts all of us involved in ministry, missions, and service: How do we set up things so that the next generation no longer needs our intervention?

Let me illustrate with a story. People were being beaten up and thrown into a river. They would float down the river until a Good Samaritan jumped in, pulled them to shore, nursed their wounds, and took them to the hospital. When going back to the river, this Good Samaritan discovered another person who had been beaten up and was floating down the river. Again, this Good Samaritan jumped in, pulled them to shore, nursed their wounds, and took them to the hospital.

But now, he tells other people about what's happening and encourages them to help. So, when the next person comes floating down the river, there are two or three more people helping pull them out of the river. Soon, there are four or five more helpers, then six, and then it's time to form a 501(c)3 non-profit "River Rescue" ministry, do some fund-raising, and buy an ambulance so they can transport all these people who are floating down the river. Next, they set up a complete program -- an efficient system -- to transport these people to the hospital. But, then, somebody asks what should have been an obvious question much earlier: *"Why are people being beaten up and thrown in the river? Shouldn't we go upriver, see what's happening, and see if maybe we can prevent this from happening in the first place?"* This is what we mean by *Prevention*.

Prevention

Prevention is our response to the question: How do we set up services so that the next generation no longer needs our intervention? Let's begin by briefly addressing a spiritual issue that frequently arises: namely, generational curses. A generational curse is a demonic spiritual stronghold that tends to affect families across generational lines. They are very real, and I've seen them manifested in many families, including my own. Generational curses often manifest through things like alcoholism, drug addiction, mental health issues, and other very real struggles that are passed from one generation to the next. These outward manifestations tend to be symptoms of deeper

> Prevention is our response to the question: How do we set up services so that the next generation no longer needs our intervention?

issues resulting from traumatic childhood experiences that are repeated from one generation to the next. While generational curses are deep rooted psychological and spiritual matters, which require mature professional counseling and pastoral guidance, our goal in this chapter is to address some of the preventative things we can do to end generational poverty from continuing from one generation to the next.

As an important side note, if you are struggling with the impacts of traumatic childhood experiences or if this book has been triggering for you, I want to encourage you to seek help from a professional licensed counselor and your pastor. If your trauma runs so deep that the thought of bringing it back up sends you into a panic, I encourage you to look into EMDR therapy as a first step, followed by traditional counseling. You did not cause your trauma, but it is your responsibility to ensure in every way possible that the generational curses passed on to you do not get passed on to the next generation. In order to do that, it takes hard work. In this, I am praying for your healing.

Now back to prevention. Prevention types of ministries are less common than intervention ministries. One example is a suicide prevention hotline where we're working to prevent that self-destructive act from happening. Another would be Big Brothers - Big Sisters, where we're mentoring at-risk kids. As was mentioned earlier in this book , studies suggest that we need to start mentoring interventions in elementary school in order to prevent a kid from dropping out of high school. In fact, 3rd grade teachers can tell you which kids are most at risk of dropping out of high school. If we wait until they're in the 10th grade, its often too late. We need to identify them in the 3rd grade and start mentoring them to prevent High School dropout and other problems further downstream. When we do dropout prevention work early, all the statistics quickly improve. Studies tell us that, if a child can make it through the 10th grade, they are probably going to graduate. But if prevention did not happen early enough, the 10th grade year is like some kind of great reckoning where dropouts happen. Why? Because kids start having holes in their education very early, before they even arrive in school.

For example, a child raised in poverty, on day-one of kindergarten, is already two months behind his Middle Class counterpart. On the first day of school, he is two-to-three months behind even without a single lesson being taught. This is due to less words being spoken to a child in poverty the first years of their life as compared to a middle class child. Without programs like Head Start, this gap continues to widen and widen with each grade level. Eventually, the child just barely makes it through 9th grade. As they look at entering 10th grade, their internal dialogue becomes something like this: I'm years behind everybody else, and I don't know what they're even talking about right now. I'm sixteen and I can get a job. My family needs the money, so I'm just going to go do that. As a result, schools get this huge dropout rate in the 10th grade. If we want to get in front of this dropout-wave, we need to do prevention work and be there with these kids in the 3rd, 4th, and 5th grades.

Advancement

We've talked about *Intervention* ministries and *Prevention* ministries. The third type of ministry we need to look at is an *Advancement* ministry. Again, like prevention, there are even fewer advancement types of ministries out there. A true *Advancement* ministry says, "Not only do we want to help you get stabilized, but we want you to grow and get ahead. We want to

> A true *Advancement* ministry says, "Not only do we want to help you get stabilized, but we want you to grow and get ahead."

be involved in helping you move forward all throughout your life." This can involve offering such things as job skills classes, resume building classes, classes on how to do a job interview, and other skills that you and I may take for granted.

A good example of an *Advancement* ministry might be Step Up Ministry, based in Raleigh, North Carolina. Step Up Ministry recognizes that 20% of the people in the Raleigh area live below the Federal Poverty Level and in some neighborhoods, 23% of the residents are unemployed. Many of these men and women are actively seeking employment and greater stability, but they face barriers such as criminal backgrounds, racial inequality, histories of drug abuse, domestic violence, and/or homelessness. Step Up works collaboratively to offer these people job training skills, such as writing resumes, developing life skills and more.[41] These kinds of advancement ministries are important because something like a professional resume can be a unique art form, but they're absolutely required to get a job that's going to pay anything close to a living wage. So, offering practical courses on things like getting your GED, or offering a financial literacy class, along with offering a lot of other different classes, fall into this area of advancement ministries. It's only after we get people stabilized that we can really look at these kinds of advancement issues. Before people get to the point of being stabilized, these kinds of things just don't work.

At Family Promise of Spokane our greatest need is not for volunteers at our shelters, but for volunteers that are willing to do the hard work of doing life with our families after we help them get housed. We serve thousands of people each year and although we have a stabilization program to help people stay housed, they need so much

Advancement takes relationships and consistent effort over an extended period of time.

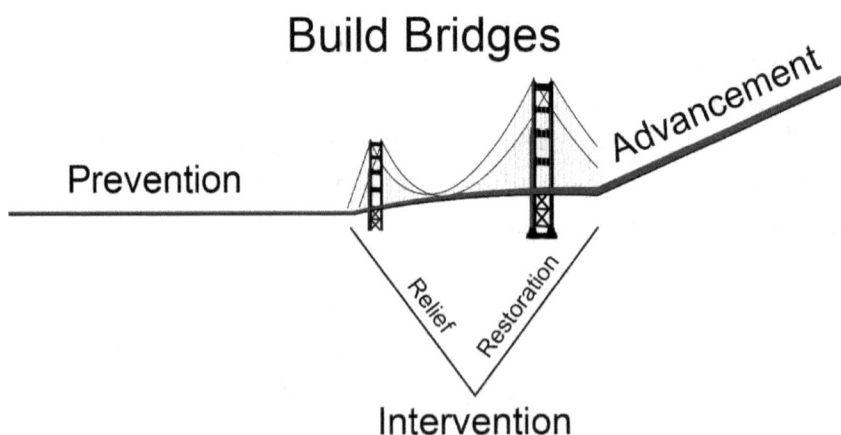

more than we can ever offer. Homelessness is not a loss of housing it is a loss of relationships. Whether someone committed sins against someone else, or sins were committed against them or just through circumstance, people experiencing homelessness have no one else to turn to, so they end up on the streets. So not only do they need to be housed they need build a new relationship network of people they can trust and lean on. This is perfect for the Church, as the only way to make disciples is to build relationship with others and do life together. However, getting churches and people in need to interact in this way is a challenge. That is because the problems are so complex and entangled that it takes a real commitment beyond just serving some food at a soup kitchen. There are so many interdependent variables that are like rungs on a ladder. You can not climb out of poverty, unless you have enough of these rungs in place at the same time, and that takes time to develop. *Advancement* takes relationships and consistent effort over an extended period of time.

Build Bridges

Prevention

Advancement

Relief

Restoration

Intervention

Going Upriver

Some other *Advancement* ministries include ESL or English as a Second Language classes. We live in a culture where it's important to be able to speak English, even though you can operate in many different languages for much of your life in the United States. Another idea along the same lines might be helping folks who become citizens by helping to navigate our legal and government systems, which is a difficult task when you speak the language and you know the culture. It can be challenging even when you work in those fields to work through the confusing processes.

Another *Advancement* ministry idea, especially in under-developed countries, might be making small, micro-loans, which tend to work better internationally than they do in the United States. There's a cultural thing that happens in other cultures where there's a *lending pool*. That pool is made up of a group of people from your whole village. If you don't pay it back, everybody in the village knows, and everybody's mad at you because they don't get any more money into the loan fund until everybody has paid back their loan. That cultural connection is very powerful. But here in the United States, we tend to be more individualistic. There's no close connection, so those lending pools don't work the same way here. They simply aren't as effective in our culture. In addition, most Americans have access to a wider variety of credit and money sources, such as payday loans, whereas a village in Africa wouldn't have any of those other resources available. Also, in America, because of all of the things that you have to work through, the startup costs for a business are much higher than those startup costs might be in a village or town in Mexico. An exception to this in the US might be in smaller immigrant communities, where the population is isolated through language and culture, and might really thrive with the help of a micro-lending pool for their community.

If we think long enough about these three stages of serving people in need (*Intervention, Prevention*, and *Advancement*), we'll eventually find ourselves asking a very basic and practical question: What can I do? What you and I need are some basic tools we can use to better understand where people are at, what they need, and how we can help them move forward. It's time to discover some tools we can use.

Reflecting And Looking Ahead

1. Reflecting on this chapter, what did you learn about serving people in need that you did not know before?

2. Based on what you learned in this chapter, how would you characterize your church or ministry outreach efforts: Intervention, Prevention, or Advancement? Explain.

3. Discuss the following statement from chapter 16: "When it comes to missions, by and large, churches tend to have a significant bias towards intervention. We intervene in difficult situations. We come in and we do things for people." Do you agree or disagree?

For Additional Study

For additional individual or group study, including a more in-depth look at what Scripture teaches on this topic, see the Study Guide for this book.

17

Tools You Can Use

"... to equip the saints for the work of ministry, for building up the body of Christ, until we all attain the unity of the faith and of the knowledge of the Son of God, to mature manhood, to the measure of the stature of the fullness of Christ." (Ephesians 4:12-13)

We've walked through the Ghetto and gotten to know our neighbors in poverty. We have gone back to the Garden and seen where poverty started. And we have explored the Gospel and how the good news creates heart change and motivates our actions. But practically, how do we take this knowledge and apply it to actually engage those in need? When we get to know our neighbors, we discover that they lack resources and have real needs. Those needs can be spiritual needs, but they can, and often do, include other needs beyond the spiritual. So, our next step is to assess what needs our neighbors have in order to understand how we might be able to work with them.

The Hand Assessment

The first tool we're going to use is something we call the Hand Assessment. Take a look at your own hand. Using your hand as a visual cue, I'm going to show you a very basic assessment you can do of anyone's needs and resources simply. The reason I like this tool is because no matter where you are, your hands are always there with you. You don't need paper or a computer. There's no fancy scoring matrix. It's just a basic needs assessment by simply using your hands and fingers as reference points. Here is how it works. When you're talking to someone in need, you can begin to get a basic idea of the different categories of needs they might have, along with what resources they have to work with. Everything I am about to say is summarized in the Hand Assessment Tool illustration on the next page. [42]

Each part of the hand represents a different resource. Let's go step by step through this tool while you think about someone you know that is in need. If you can not think of someone now, think about an impoverished character from a movie you have seen. When discussing each category think about if the person you are thinking of has a lot of that resource, an average amount, or very little of that resource. Keep that in mind and when we get to the end I will ask you to create a list of resources the person you are thinking of needs and how they might gain them.

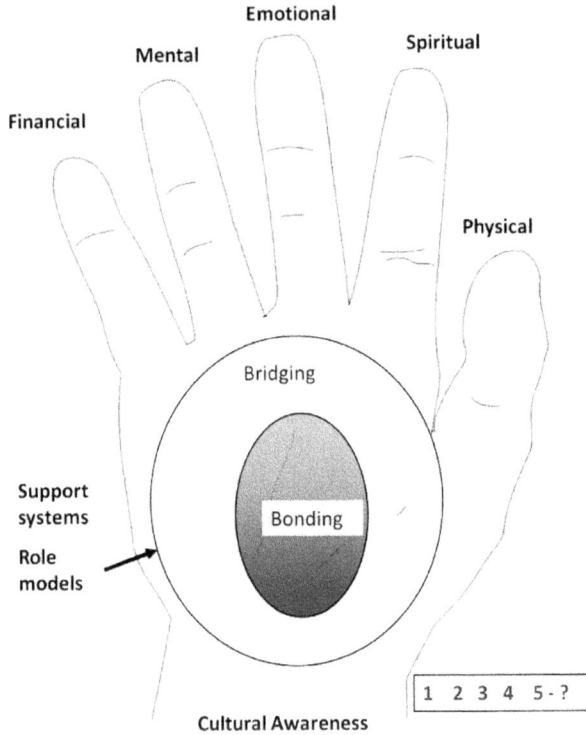

Thumb = Physical Resources: The Thumb represents physical resources, such as someone's physical health and their ability to physically do things. For example, if the person you're assessing is physically disabled, then they would have a low physical resource score.

Index Finger = Spiritual Resources: The Index Finger, or the pointer finger, represents spiritual resources. The Index Finger points up or the way towards more spiritual resources.

Interestingly, when creating this model it was people living in generational poverty that selected the index finger to represent spiritual resources. When asked why, they said, *"Because that's the most important one to me."* Let that sink in for just a minute. People in generational poverty said that was the most important resource to them. When prayer is all you have, you use it daily for survival. Often. Churches from Middle Class communities will send a missions team into a poor community or country with the assumption that they are going

> When prayer is all you have, you use it daily for survival.

to save the people there. Sometimes that is the case, but more often the mission's team discovers people in poverty who are far more faithful and stronger believers than them! Financial wealth does not equal spiritual wealth and financial poverty does not equal spiritual poverty. I have met people experiencing homelessness who said to me, "This is my most important asset because that's the only one I have. I didn't know it was the only one I needed until it was the only one I had."

Middle Finger = Emotional Resources: The Middle Finger represents emotional resources. When this tool was originally designed, a middle class social worker categorized the ring finger as representing emotional resources. The thinking was that weddings and marriage elicited emotions. Then, as it was taught to people in generational poverty, they said, *"Oh, that's not the emotional finger. I'll show you the emotional finger."* So, by popular demand, the Middle Finger is now the emotional finger in this model, which represents someone's ability to identify and navigate their emotions well through different circumstances.

Ring Finger = Mental Resources: The Ring Finger represents mental resources. There's really no reason for this choice, other than we're running out of fingers to choose from! This represents your ability to think and process through situations and to gain new knowledge.

Pinky Finger = Financial Resources: The Pinky Finger represents financial resources. Once again, folks in poverty actually put this one there. Why did they put financial resources on the pinky? Because, according to them, it's the weakest and the smallest. Folks living in generational poverty said it's the one that, sometimes, they could do without. Let's face it. That response seems counter-intuitive. It's counter intuitive because when we try to fight poverty, we do so by throwing money at the problem. But it's people living in generational poverty telling us that, money would be nice and they will take it, but when it comes down to it these other resources are more important than money. We will often hear people in poverty say something like, "I have lived my whole life without money and I have still survived."

Wrist = *Cultural Awareness:* The Wrist represents cultural awareness. This is an adaptation from the original model which did not include this, but we felt it is vital to have cultural awareness, which is a person's ability to navigate through different environments. After working with people living in Povertyville, we noticed that they had to work in Middle Classburg. In order to do that, they had to adapt their resources to effectively work in a Middle Class environment. Those who could do that well usually did better and could hold jobs longer. For example, if a friend calls me on my cell phone, I might answer , "Hey what's up." If I have my new job and someone calls my work and I pick up the phone and say, "Hey, what's up," does that go over very well with my new employer? No, probably not. Cultural awareness means I'm able to navigate resources depending on the environment, along with things like how you present yourself in different situations and in different cultures. What you put on a resume, what you wear to a job interview, and what you say to a customer are all cultural habits that can be learned, and your awareness of those is a critical component of success in a Middle Class workplace environment.

Center of the Palm = *Bonding Relationships:* The middle part of the palm represents what we call bonding relationships. These are the relationships with the people who are the closest to you. They can't really help you get ahead, but they help you get by. These are your close, close, close friends, family, and relationships. Your bonding relationships are usually with people who are in the same socio-economic state as you and you rely on one another daily to get by.

Palm between center and fingers = *Bridging Relationships:* Between the palm and the fingers are relationships called bridging relationships. These relationships are with people who can connect you to more resources. For example, a teacher might be a bridging relationship to more mental resources. If I needed more physical resources, a coach or a physical therapist might help me gain more resources physically. A pastor would be a bridging relationship to more spiritual resources. A counselor might be a bridging relationship to more emotional resources. These people are bridges from where we are to greater knowledge and ability in one or more of these areas.

What we often see in cultures of poverty are people who have really close bonding relationships but usually don't have a lot of bridging relationships. As a result, people in generational poverty are good at staying where they are, but they often don't have the relationships that can help them get ahead.

Alright, now that you know what each part of the hand represents, I want you to come back to the thinking about the person you know from a poverty background and go through each category while looking at your hand. Would you rate them high, medium, or low on physical resources? Spiritual? Emotional? Mental? Financial? Cultural Awareness? Bonding Relationships? Bridging Relationships? Now, after you have thought through each of these take the categories they are low in and think about what type of relationship they need to gain more of a particular resource. How could you help introduce them to this bridging relationship?

Great, now before you go any further you need to speak with the person in need and ask if they would like help meeting someone that can help with gaining more of that resource. If they agree, now you can help make those connections.

Resource Table

The next tool I want to equip you with is a Resources Table. This table corresponds with the categories in the Hand Assessment and provides recommended tools and techniques which can be used to overcome the barriers that exist to gaining more resources.

Let's take a brief look at what the table can tell us. For example, the table tells us that folks in generational poverty tend to highly value spiritual resources. Sometimes, all you can do for people stuck in generational poverty is pray for them. Prayer is not an insignificant resource, either for them or for us. For them prayer represents hope. For us, prayer represents the potential for God's intervening and transforming power to change circumstances and to transform lives and communities. The table also tells us that residents of Middle Classburg tend to regard spiritual resources as more of a transactional thing. "I'll work really hard so that God will give me (BLANK)." For the Christian, the table reminds us that spiritual resources are central and are focused on God's love for us and others.

A Resources Table

Resources	Relationship (Social & Spiritual)	Mental (Language)	Emotional	Physical (Food)	Financial
Povertyville, USA	Highly Valued	Casual Register Language of Survival	Power & Respect are things to fight for.	Quantity is Key "Did you have enough?	Money is to be used & spent. Impulsivity
Middle Classburg, America	Transactional	Formal Register Language of Negotiation	Power & Respect are Separate	Quality is Key "Did you like it?"	Money is to be managed.
Christian	Central. Focused on God's Love.	Uses All Registers. Use Language to communicate	Power & Respect are in Christ. Holy Spirit gives power to serve others	Gratitude & Contentment are Key. "Am I thankful?"	Money is a stewardship. All money is God's. We are His Stewards.
Tools	1. Testimony: Share Your Story 2. Evangelism: Share God's Story. 3. Discipleship: Share your life (Mentor)	1. Teach A Formal Register 2. Be Aware of Non-Verbals. 3. Rewrite Forms. 4. Do Hands-On Training 5. Tell Stories 6. Use Drawings & Models	1. How can I serve someone else in this situation? 2. If you choose (BLANK), then you have chosen (BLANK).	1. Be Thankful 2. Model Healthy Relationships 3. Discuss Healthy Eating Habits.	1. Pray Over Your Money 2. Have Written Daily Goals. 3. Teach Working Backwards.

There are three main tools you can use to help someone gain more spiritual resources. *First,* you can share your story. Your story of life-change through the knowledge and acceptance of Jesus Christ is your testimony. Your testimony should cover three areas: This is what my life was like before I knew the Lord. This is how I came to know and accept Jesus as my Lord and Savior. This is what my life is like afterwards.

A *second* tool you can use is to share God's story. This is called evangelism and is sharing the story of how God acted through Christ to save the world as it is recorded in the Bible. This is the good news for those who are living in a broken world, which is everyone.

The *third* tool is to share your life. This is what the Bible calls discipleship.

The word disciple simply means a follower. Let me spend some time discussing discipleship. The very last thing that Christ says while He is on earth, as recorded in Matthew 28: 18-20, is a command to go and make disciples. This is God commanding us to go and make followers. One of the most effective ways to do this is to invite another person into a relationship where you are saying to the other person, "Come, follow me as I follow God."

In my experience, this is by far the tool we use the least in leading others to a saving knowledge of Jesus Christ. Think about it. We read in the Scriptures about Jesus, the disciples, and the Apostle Paul all going to people and saying something like, "Follow me." But we rarely do the same. We say things like, "Come

> Discipleship means inviting someone into your life, just like Jesus did.

to my Church," or "Read this book," or maybe even, "Do this Bible Study." But when was the last time you said to someone, "Come, follow me." If you want to see lives and communities changed in dramatic ways, it's going to take believers who invite others to "come and follow." Now, on a practical level, you may be thinking, I just don't have time to add another thing to my calendar. I have work, kids sports, and I have to make dinner. I just don't have extra time. If you are like most Americans you're absolutely right! You don't have the time to add more things to your already hectic schedule. This is why you shouldn't be thinking about adding another meeting to your schedule. You should think about adding someone to your life. You are already going to be having meetings, coaching kids sports and making dinner, just invite someone else along with you to do those things. Follow me as I do my work. Follow me as I coach my kids sports. Follow me as we make and eat dinner. This is what I mean by discipleship.

A Simple Discipleship Paradigm.
One of my favorite discipleship paradigms works like this:
  Step 1: You invite someone into a relationship and say, "Come follow me."
  Step 2: The first time you do something, you do it, they watch, and then you explain why you did it that way.
  Step 3: The next time, you do it, they help you do it, and you explain why you did it that way.
  Step 4: The third time around, they do it, you help them do it, and they explain to you why they did it that way.

Step 5: This time, they do it, you watch them do it, and they explain why they did it that way

Step 6: They invite somebody else to do the same thing, and the process starts all over again.

The reason I love this particular structure (I do, you watch. I do, you help. You do, I help. You do, I watch. You invite somebody else) is because it works in almost any mentoring/teaching situation, from fixing a car, to leading a Bible Study, to parenting a child. Also when somebody's watching you, you actually think about why you do what you do! Genuine discipleship doesn't have to be a "meeting" reading a book. In fact, it's better if it's not a meeting, particularly for younger people and those in poverty. Jesus never invited anyone to a discipleship meeting. His life was the meeting, and He simply said, "Come and see" (John 1:39). Discipleship means inviting someone into your life, just like Jesus did. Don't invite them into your calendar; invite them into your life.

Mental Resources. The next resource on our *Resources Table* is *Mental Resources*. An important mental resource is language and our ability to communicate. People in generational poverty tend to use something known as a casual register. A casual register describes the way you and I would talk with friends -- situations where word choice isn't specific. In casual register, our non-verbals communicate our story more than what we're saying.

In Middle Class, we use what's called a formal register. In formal register, word choice is really important. We don't say, "I used to went over there," but "I used to go over there." A formal register consists of very specific word choices (think proper grammar and word choice, rather than street slang). As Christians, we use both registers and more (such as specialized theological terms). Some things we say the exact same way every time. Some things come from our casual register, and other things come from our formal register. But it's all about communicating in such a way that we communicate God's glory for the good of others.

In the United States, all of our communication structures run off of a formal register. Our educational system, our business system, our legal system -- our whole society runs off of a formal register. That's why we have to teach a particular way of speaking. You need to realize that folks living in generational poverty often don't use formal register. They may not have a large

> In the United States, all of our communication structures run off of a formal register.

vocabulary, and for many of them, English is a second language. However, this does not mean that they are any less intelligent than someone from middle class. Your vocabulary does not equal your intelligence. If we make the mistake of confusing vocabulary with intelligence, we will wrongly conclude that, because of how someone communicates, that this person is not intelligent. Nothing could be further from the truth! They simply haven't learned our register. They haven't learned those particular vocabulary words and how to use them in the correct setting. Often immigrants and refugees will be discredited or discounted on jobs or opportunities because of their verbal skills, even though their intelligence is more than able to accomplish whatever the job-task might be. This is why we need to teach people to speak and write in formal register.

We also need to be very aware of our non-verbals. We need to understand that people in generational poverty are experts at reading non-verbals. This isn't about what you say. It's about how you say what you say. For example, if I'm living in generational poverty, I might walk up to my friend and say, "Hey, Jamie, what's happening jerk? " Then we laugh, shake hands and I pull him in for a one arm hug. On the other hand, I might walk up to someone I am upset with and say, "Hey, Jamie, what's happening jerk?" however this time my face is stern, my chest is puffed out and my hands are clinched in fists. I've just used the exact same words, but they have two different meanings based on my non-verbals. This is why, when you're speaking to somebody from generational poverty, if you're using the wrong facial expression or body language, they will know if your words are true or not They are reading how you say what you say, not just what you say.

> We need to understand that people in generational poverty are experts at reading non-verbals.

Think about it like this. If you have ever been to another culture where they speak a different language, and you don't know that language, how much more do you add hand motions to your words? Remember, folks in generational poverty tend to speak with a lot more hand motions and large dramatic movements. Sometimes, when you see two people from generational poverty talking their hand movements are so large that it is difficult to tell if they're just talking or if they're getting ready to fight! So, be extra aware of your non-verbals.

Bilateral Conversations Versus Participatory Storytelling. In Middle Classburg, America, we tend to have bilateral conversations. Meaning we take turns speaking. I say something and you listen quietly until I finish. Then you speak and I listen. But I'm not really listening to understand what you're saying. I'm listening to figure out how I'm going to respond to what you're saying. When you finish speaking, I respond and you get to listen. Also, in Middle Classburg, America, we tend to take a face-to-face posture when we talk to each other. Conversely, when you're working with someone in generational poverty conversations are more like a story that we tell together. The other person starts telling a story, and then I jump in on it, and then he tells me more, and I make a comment it's more like group effort or a dance that we do together, rather than you go, I go, you go, I go. Also, since face-to-face is a confrontational posture. The posture we are in when we fight, in generational poverty we are usually at an angle to the person we are talking with.

There's a hidden danger for those of us in Middle Classburg when it comes to this type of communication. Often, someone in generational poverty will be telling us something that they think is very important, but they're going off on tangents while they work their way around to their point. For our part, we stand there quietly and patiently listening to them. They finish and we respond. We think we did a great job of listening to their whole story patiently and politely before responding. However, the other person walks away and saying to themselves, "That person is a jerk! They didn't listen to me at all! They didn't engage, they didn't interact!" Same conversation, but two very different takeaways. Why? Because we failed to understand the importance of non-verbals like big hand motions or even a simple hand or touch on the shoulder that says, "Hey, I'm listening." Also we didn't jump in with verbal acknowledgments enough like, "No Way," "Really," "Tell me more." Remember to use your non-verbals. Be aware of them, and don't try to be too cool with your slang vocabulary (we generally aren't very good at it). Simply be who you are, but be aware of where you are and who you're talking to. I want to touch on few more of these tools in your *Resources Table* before we move on to discuss *The Needs Ladder*.

Rewrite Forms. Another helpful practice is to rewrite forms to make them easier to understand. We live in world so afraid of lawsuits that our forms are full of legal language that is hard for anyone to understand. For people with limited vocabulary these forms can make someone feel like they are being taken advantage of because they don't understand. A simple fix to this is to add a sentence above each legal section that describes that section in plain simple terms. Examples could say something like, "The next section says its ok for us to take your picture for our records," or "This says if you get hurt we can take you to the doctor."

Hands-On Training. Whenever possible, do hands-on training or on-the-job training. More often than not, formal classes or workshops don't work very well for people from generational poverty backgrounds. It usually works a lot better to be hands-on, where we work together on a task. We're actually doing something, rather than sitting in a room, listening to someone lecture.

Tell stories. Why? Because, the story teaches the lesson. For example, when I was in high school, my football coach was also the local coroner (I know, that's a great combo of professions.). Well, one day he came to practice and tells us how they had gotten a call to respond to a milk-processing plant to pickup a dead body. At this milk-processing plant they had these giant blenders where they mixed the milk and they had posted a sign on the wall that said:

UNPLUG MACHINE BEFORE CLEANING.

But somebody forgot to unplug the machine. As they were reaching into the big blender to clean it, they fell in. And as they fell they kicked the switch and blended themselves. Pieces of the body were everywhere.

So, now, when they do the training at that facility, they tell that story, and how they found a finger on the rafters two months later. Guess what. NO ONE forgets to unplug the machine anymore. Why? Because, *the story teaches the lesson.* The story teaches the lesson, not the sign. With a lesson like that, who needs a sign?!

> The story teaches the lesson.

Jesus never worked at the milk-processing plant, but He understood the power of storytelling. He told parables, stories drawn from everyday life and experience in 1st century Israel, each of which makes a specific point. Our minds are designed to grab onto stories and to hold on to those stories for life.

Use Drawings And Models. Learn to use and work with drawings and models. If you have ever shopped at IKEA or built a lego set, you already know how effective drawings can be. IKEA is the largest furniture store in the world. You walk in and say, "I love that bookshelf! ! I'm going to take that bookshelf home!" They respond to your enthusiasm by giving you a box. You take that box home, open it up and discover forty-eight parts and a set of instructions with no words! Just drawings. But, amazingly, you and people in countries all over the world are able to put that same piece of furniture together with nothing more than drawings. So, use drawings (and models) to better communicate ideas and to help people understand, rather than relying on writing things out.

Emotional Resources. I want to spend a few minutes on the topic of Emotional Resources. In Povertyville, USA, power and respect are the same thing. They can't be separated. That means you don't give someone power over you if you don't respect them. But in Middle Classburg, America, it's not the same. We may not respect our boss, but we acknowledge that he or she has authority over us. In Middle Classburg, we separate power from respect. In Povertyville, they're the same thing. This means, if your boss is a jerk and you live in Povertyville, you may utilize your Emotional Finger, and quit by walking out the door. But, if you're a resident of Middle Classburg and your boss is a jerk, what do you do before you quit your job? You find another job. And you probably skip using the emotional finger, choosing instead to write a really nice letter thanking him for giving you the opportunity to learn so much while working there (all the while thinking that you should have gone with the finger. Why do you write this nice letter? Because you don't want to burn the bridge. But in Povertyville, things work a little differently. I once saw someone quit a job at Burger King because of the way another employee, who was not her boss, talked to her. She felt disrespected and said, "That's it! I'm out of here."

As Christians, we're to have a different view on this. Power and respect belong to the Lord, and ultimately, we work for Him. He gives us power by the Holy Spirit, Who enables us to serve others. Our calling is to ask ourselves how we can serve others in this situation. Serving others becomes a teaching tool in our ministry. That means, when we're working with someone, our ministry task is to ask them, How can you serve someone else in this situation? The issue isn't whether they are a good boss or a bad boss, but how we can serve them in this particular situation.

Choices And Consequences. Another important ministry tool has to do with teaching those we work with about the relationship between choices and consequences. For example, it might go something like this: "If you choose X, then you are also choosing Y." In practical terms, you might say: "If you choose to write your paper, then you are also choosing to take your brother to Disneyland. And if you choose not to write your paper, then you are choosing not to take your brother to Disneyland." Their most likely response will be to say, "What?" And that's when this conversation becomes a teachable moment. Now you can say something like this:

"Look, if you choose to write that paper, you're going to pass this class. And if you pass this class, you're going to go on to the next grade, and then, eventually, you're going to graduate. And if you graduate high school, you will make $5,000 more a year than if you didn't graduate. And for $5,000, you could take your brother and the whole family to Disneyland!"

You are now teaching this person the relationship between choices and consequences by relating it to something that's important to them: their relationship with their brother and family. If I had just said, "If you don't write this paper, you're not going to pass this class," that same child would probably have said, "Yeah? So what? I don't care. That's not important to me." We've changed the dynamic of the conversation because achievement is no longer the important thing. Now it's all about an important relationship.

The Ladder of Stability

The *Ladder of Stability* is a graphic I created several years ago to illustrate a point. The ladder shows how many different categories of resources are involved just to get someone to stable ground. The ladder starts (yes, bottom rung) with basic needs, such as food, clothing, and housing. These are basic physical resources for our survival. Then the ladder goes on to highlight resources: language, health and healthcare, substance abuse treatment, social support, and emotional and spiritual support. Then there are things like parenting skills, childcare, education, legal and identification. Often when people loose everything they also loose their identification. Think about it this way, if there was a fire today and your home burned to the ground, would you have your social security card? Would you have your children's birth certificates? No, and likely you would have a hard time remembering your kids social security numbers. However, you will need that to get help. You will need your social

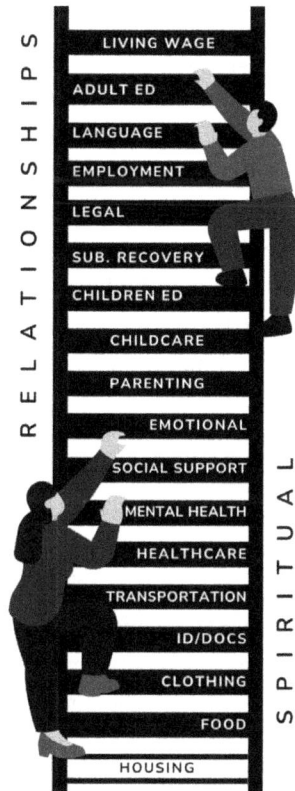

The ladder rungs from top to bottom: LIVING WAGE, ADULT ED, LANGUAGE, EMPLOYMENT, LEGAL, SUB. RECOVERY, CHILDREN ED, CHILDCARE, PARENTING, EMOTIONAL, SOCIAL SUPPORT, MENTAL HEALTH, HEALTHCARE, TRANSPORTATION, ID/DOCS, CLOTHING, FOOD, HOUSING. Left side: RELATIONSHIPS. Right side: SPIRITUAL.

security number to apply for a job or fill out an application for an apartment. In fact, a homeless person knowing their and their children's social security numbers is one of the largest factors in determining if they will get into housing. In order to get to stable ground, you have to have a stable job with a living wage. But you can't have a stable job with a living wage without proper identification. So, if you don't have any ID, we must take care of that need before you can even get to the job part. We could do all the job training we want, but if we haven't solved the ID problem, we can't get to that next step. Next, not only do you need to be employed, but you need to earn a living wage.

You might be able to skip a step here or there, but most of these nineteen steps need to be in place for someone to achieve stability. The *Ladder of Stability* reveals an important reality. When we're talking about all these issues, we suddenly realize that there's no way any one organization or group can solve all these problems. That means we need to partner. It means your church needs to partner with other agencies and organizations that do these different things. You, your church, or your ministry need to identify what resources you can bring to the table, and then you need to figure out who you can partner with for all the other things that are needed by the people you are working with.

But there's a catch with this ladder. In reality it functions more like a rope ladder than a solid ladder. In fact, it resembles that Jacob's Ladder game you might have seen at a carnival. The game looks pretty simple, all you have to do is take six steps and then ring the bell at the other end. Easy, right? If you do it, they'll give you the biggest prize at the Fair for that one game. That is because it's really the most difficult game of all. Two or three steps into it and something happens. You get off-balance. The ladder flips over. You're done. And you walk away thinking, It really didn't look that hard.

That's exactly the way life is in poverty. You get two or three things going and then something unexpected happens. The ladder flips over. Something breaks down with your car, or you get sick, or your child gets in trouble, or one of your family members flips the ladder over on you. Suddenly, you find yourself being pulled back into Povertyville, just when you thought you were making progress getting out.

Finally, relationships and spiritual resources are the two rails which hold the entire ladder tightly together. You need people to help you, to pray for you, and to hold the ladder tight so you can climb up. You're not climbing up for them, but you need them to help hold those resources together so you can take the next step, achieve, and get ahead.

The Role of the Church

And this brings us to our last point for this chapter. The body of believers -- the Church -- is the only organization in the community large enough to have relationships with every single person who's in need. The Church is the only one. There's never going to be enough teachers; there's never going to be enough social workers; and there's never going to be enough counselors, or police officers or other professionals to have relationships with every person who's in need. But God has designed His Church to be big enough to do it. And it's the only group with a divinely-imparted mission to go and make disciples. And making disciples requires that we build relationships. You cannot make a disciple without having a relationship with someone, right? You cannot make a follower of Christ without having a relationship with somebody. If you walk away with anything from this chapter, walk away with this: Each of us needs to build meaningful relationships with people in need. It's how I can love God with all my heart, mind, soul, and strength and love my neighbor as myself, just as Jesus commanded. From there, all I need is to figure out what I can do to serve them, without doing it for them.

Reflecting and Looking Ahead

1. Reflecting on this chapter, what one practical tool did you discover that will help you better understand and serve someone working their way out of generational poverty?

2. What did you learn from the "Hand Assessment Tool" that was a new insight for you? How did this tool help you better understand the mindset of people in generational poverty and how to approach working with them?

3. Referring to the "Resources Table," the author talked about the difference between a discipleship paradigm that says "Come to my church," and one which says "Come, follow me." Which paradigm are you using? Why?

For Additional Study
For additional individual or group study, including a more in-depth look at what Scripture teaches on this topic, see the Study Guide for this book.

18
From Knowledge to Action

When we started this journey through the Ghetto, the Garden, and the Gospel I asked you to read with an open and curious mind as you seek to learn, just as we are. Our journey has taken us on a path that bridges the historical, social, and spiritual dimensions of poverty, revealing not only its complexities but also the profound responsibility we, as Christians, hold in addressing it. Now as I refresh what we have learned I want us to consider this question, "What am I going to do with this knowledge?" Knowledge is not enough, it is the application of knowledge that changes the world.

The Heart of Poverty: Broken Relationships

Poverty is more than a lack of financial resources; it is a symptom of broken relationships - with God, with ourselves, with others, and with creation. This understanding reframes our approach from mere charity to holistic restoration.

Understanding Poverty: Beyond Monetary Measures

Traditional definitions of poverty, such as the Federal Poverty Level, fall short in capturing its true essence. Poverty is not just about lacking money; it's about lacking the resources necessary to maintain a stable environment, including education, healthcare, employment, and supportive relationships.

The Journey Through Middle Classburg and Povertyville

By metaphorically trading places between Middle Classburg, America, and Povertyville, USA, we gained a deeper appreciation of the systemic barriers faced by those in poverty. The interconnectedness of issues such as transportation, employment, housing, and healthcare became evident, underscoring the necessity of comprehensive solutions.

The Biblical Mandate: Compassion and Justice

The biblical mandate to serve "the least of these" calls us not only to charity, but to action. We should strive for systemic changes that uplift the marginalized and restores dignity. The Gospel compels us to act justly, love mercy, and walk humbly with our God.

The Transformative Power of Community

Effective poverty alleviation is rooted in relationships. Building genuine, empathetic connections with those we seek to help transforms both the helper and the helped.

A Call to Action: Steps Toward Lasting Impact

At this point you may be thinking to yourself, "Ok, but really, how can I as one person actually make a significant difference?" Well, it is not easy, in fact it is hard, it is the type of hard that produces tangible results. Nothing worthwhile is ever really easy. But it is worth it! The following steps should help to get you started.

1. Build Relationships: Engage with those experiencing poverty. Listen to their stories, understand their needs, and build trust. Relationships are the foundation of effective support. If you don't know how to connect with those in generational poverty, then start volunteering at an organization that serves those in need and meet the people they serve.

2. Advocate for Change: Use your voice to advocate for policies that address systemic issues contributing to poverty. Support initiatives that promote affordable housing, healthcare, education, and decent wages and fight injustice. Be the voice for someone that has no voice.

Julia's Story

One of our first families when we opened the Family Emergency Shelter in 2016 was a family with two little girls. The oldest girl was named Julie. She had just started school for the first time and she was learning how to write her name. I would see her and we would make silly faces and sometimes I would color with her. After a little while the family found an apartment and we helped them get a lease. The parents who had been homeless for most of their lives, and nearly all of their daughter's lives, were so proud and excited to finally have a place of their own.

On moving day, the mom stops by my office and says, "Julie wanted to write a thank you card and give it to you." So this little girl comes in and she hands me a little sticky note. On that sticky note it read, "Julia, Julia, julia julia julia. Julia julia julia. Julia." You see, she only knew how to write her name. She obviously wanted to express more, but she did not have the words, so she just repeated her name.

This note is important to me because it is a reminder that we represent homeless children and they have no voice. They do not get to express their needs, it's not safe to have children downtown or on the street corners, so they are overlooked by our government and our communities when it comes to thinking about the homeless. In fact if you ask someone to describe a homeless person, 99% of the time they describe a homeless adult, usually a man. However, children make up 36% of the homeless in the US.

Since kids have even less of a voice than adults, it impacts funding. In fact, a child in our shelter in 2022 received 843% less funding from our local government than a man staying in a single adult shelter in the same community. Are our kids really 843% less valuable? I hope not, because these kids, without intervention now, are the most likely future street homeless.

What we see in our downtowns and what we are spending so much money on is what we didn't do for kids 10 to 15 years ago. For this reason, the children we serve need our voice. All those who are marginalized need a voice, they need your voice. They are relying not just on your donations, but also on your influence. You can amplify their voices in your workplaces, your faith congregations, among your friends and family and with your elected officials.

3. Pray and Fast: Prayer is powerful. It is a direct line of communication between you and the creator of all things. Lift up prayers to God. Ask him, "Lord, what is your will for my community?" "What is my part for those in need." "How do you want me to serve them."

Also, try doing a fast like we discussed earlier in the book. The idea here is to intentionally go without something, so that others might have that. This could mean fasting from food or it could mean putting off a purchase so that you can help support an organization or someone in need.

Conclusion: Becoming the Change

As we come to the conclusion of our journey together my challenge to you is to embrace the gospel in your own life. Then with your heart set ablaze from the freedom that Christ has brought you, take that good news with you to combat complexities of poverty in your own community. Let us strive to be the hands and feet of Christ, bringing hope, healing, and transformation to a world in desperate need. Remember, how we serve the poor could have eternal consequences. The time is now. Rise to the challenge and make a difference that will echo into eternity.

The Ghetto, the Garden and the Gospel

Endnotes

1.Ruby K. Payne. *A Framework For Understanding Poverty: A Cognitive Approach, 5th Revised Edition* (aha! Process, Inc.: Highlands, TX, 2013).

2. Adapted from Ruby K. Payne. *A Framework For Understanding Poverty: A Cognitive Approach, 5th Revised Edition* (aha! Process, Inc.: Highlands, TX, 2013).

3. Ibid., 45.

4. In 1996, Extreme Poverty was originally defined as $1.00 per day. The international definition is occasionally adjusted for inflation and international price changes. In 2017 the World Bank defined Extreme Poverty as living below $1.90 a day, measured in 2011 international prices. Subsequently, that number has been adjusted to $2.15 in 2017 prices, and $2.47 in 2022 prices. See also, Joe Hasell (2022) - "From $1.90 to $2.15 a day: the updated International Poverty Line" Published online at OurWorldInData.org. Retrieved from: 'https://ourworldindata.org/from-1-90-to-2-15-a-day-the-updated-international-poverty-line'

5. Source: The World Bank @ https://data.worldbank.org/topic/11. Our thanks to Dr. Amanda C. Nothaft, PhD, Director of Data and Evaluation, Poverty Solutions at the University of Michigan for her assistance in providing poverty data research and directing us to the World Bank as a primary source. For more on Extreme Poverty see, Lauren Feeney, "Living On $2 A Day: Exploring Extreme Poverty in America," Posted Dec 27, 2015 11:30 AM EDT @ https://www.pbs.org/newshour/nation/poverty.

6. In 2020 the World Bank estimated that the number of those experiencing extreme poverty in the United States was .25% (on a population of 331.5 million from the 2020 Census, or about 828,623 people). Source: World Bank @ https://pip.worldbank.org/country-profiles/USA.

7. This original map from the *Dallas Morning News* has not been subsequently updated. For updated poverty rates in Dallas and elsewhere in Texas, see Michael Mooney, "Poverty In Texas, mapped," at https://www.axios.com/local/dallas/2022/04/15/texas-poverty-map

8. The term gentrification was first coined in the 1960s by British sociologist Ruth Glass in her book, *London: Aspects of Change*. Gentrification describes a process of urban renewal, development, or transformation brought about by the buying and renovating of houses, buildings, and stores in deteriorated urban neighborhoods. While gentrification can renew urban areas and raise property values, it can also force the displacement of low-income families and small businesses.

9. Merton, Robert K. "The Unanticipated Consequences of Purposive Social Action." *American Sociological Review* 1, no. 6 (1936): 894–904. https://doi.org/10.2307/2084615

10. You can view President Johnson's "War On Poverty" speech at https://youtu.be/f3AuStymweQ.

11. Learn more about Mollie Orshansky online at https://www.ssa.gov/policy/docs/ssb/v68n3/v68n3p79.html.

12. A more detailed analysis is available from the UC-Davis, "What is the current poverty rate in the United States?" at
https://poverty.ucdavis.edu/faq/what-current-poverty-rate-united-states.
Total spending on poverty related programs by the Federal Government is a source of debate, as seen here, "No, We Don't Spend $1 Trillion On Welfare Each Year" posted online at https://www.washingtonpost.com/.
See also "The American Welfare State: How We Spend Nearly $1 Trillion a Year Fighting Poverty—And Fail," posted online at https://www.cato.org.

13. Vance Ginn, Ph.D., "We Know What Works in the War on Poverty," at Texas Public Policy Foundation, published May 6, 2022. Accessed March 26, 2024 @
https://www.texaspolicy.com/we-know-what-works-in-the-war-on-poverty/

14. A quick reference table of year-by-year poverty percentages and numbers is available here: https://www.healthcare.gov/glossary/federal-poverty-level-fpl/ More detailed analysis is available from the UC-Davis, "What is the current poverty rate in the United States?" at https://poverty.ucdavis.edu/faq/what-current-poverty-rate-united-states. Total spending on poverty related programs by the Federal Government is a source of debate. See "No, We Don't Spend $1 Trillion On Welfare Each Year" posted online at https://www.washingtonpost.com/. See also "The American Welfare State: How We Spend Nearly $1 Trillion a Year Fighting Poverty—And Fail," posted online at https://www.cato.org.

15. "Why Is Homelessness Increasing." Washington State Department of Commerce. http://www.commerce.wa.gov/wp-content/uploads/2017/01/hau-why-homelessness-increase-2017.pdf (Retrieved February 28, 2019).

16. "Just five states (California, New York, Florida, Washington, and Texas) account for 55 percent of people experiencing homelessness. And only 25 Continuums of Care (CoCs) account for 47 percent of all homelessness." More data on this can be found at: https://endhomelessness.org/homelessness-in-america/homelessness-statistics/state-of-homelessness/

17. For more on the relationship between homelessness, poverty, and housing, see Gregg Colburn and Clayton Page Aldern, *Homelessness Is A Housing Problem* (University of California Press; First edition March 15, 2022. ISBN: 978-0520383784.

18. According to Hedges & Company the average age of cars on the road in 2023 was 13.7 years, up 2.3 years over the past 10 years.
https://hedgescompany.com/blog/2024/02/average-age-of-cars-trucks/

19. Amy K. Glasmeier, "Living Wage Calculator," Massachusetts Institute of Technology, 2024. Accessed on April 3, 2023, https://livingwage.mit.edu/counties/53063

20. Kevin Van Paassen. "Good Health Depends on Wealth, New Canadian Report Finds." The Globe and Mail, July 30, 2013. Accessed April 3, 2024 @
https://www.theglobeandmail.com/life/health-and-fitness/health/good-health-depends-on-wealth-new-canadian-report-finds/article13513490/ Additional studies in recent years have also noted the relationship between good health and wealth (or financial stability). See Elaine

St.Peter, "Wealthy, Healthy - Changes in wealth linked to changes in cardiovascular health," Harvard Medical School, June 30, 2021. Accessed April 3, 2024. https://hms.harvard.edu/news/wealthy-healthy. See also, Kim Krisberg, "Income inequality: When wealth determines health: Earnings influential as lifelong social determinant of health," The Nation's Health, October 2016, 46 (8) 1-17. Accessed April 3, 2024. https://www.thenationshealth.org/content/46/8/1.1.

21. Learn more about ACEs @ https://www.cdc.gov/violenceprevention/aces/about.html

22. You can take the ACEs survey for yourself at: https://acestoohigh.com/got-your-ace-score/

23. In a May, 2017 interview, Housing and Urban Development Secretary Ben Carson got himself into hot water by saying that a "certain mindset" contributes to people living in poverty, suggesting that children take that mindset from their parents at a young age. While you and I might not agree with everything Secretary Carson said in his interview, what he was essentially describing is a "mindset" of generational poverty. Jose A. DelReal. "Ben Carson Calls Poverty 'A State of Mind' During Interview." The Washington Post. https://www.washingtonpost.com/news/post-politics/wp/2017/05/24/ben-carson-calls-poverty-a -state-of-mind-during-interview/ (Retrieved February 28, 2019).

24. Reuven Feuerstein et al., *Instrumental Enrichment*, in *A Framework For Understanding Poverty: A Cognitive Approach*, Ruby K. Payne, 5th Revised Edition (Highlands, TX: aha! Process, Inc., 2013), p.122.

25. You can find Admiral McRaven's commencement address on YouTube. It also available as a book: William H. McRaven. *Make Your Bed: Little Things That Can Change Your Life...And Maybe the World*. 2nd edition. Grand Central Publishing. (April 4, 2017).

26. I have adapted this chart from Philip E. DeVol, Ruby K. Payne, and Terie Dreussi Smith *Bridges Out of Poverty*. Revised edition 2009 (Highlands, TX: aha! Process, Inc., 2001).

27. *"Expedited Assistance For Victims Of Hurricanes Katrina And Rita: FEMA's Control Weaknesses Exposed the Government to Significant Fraud and Abuse"* Government Accounting Office. https://www.gao.gov/assets/120/112786.pdf (Retrieved February 28, 2019). See also: Jordan Weissmann, "Did Katrina Victims Really Spend Their Relief Money on Gucci Bags and Massage Parlors?" *The Atlantic*. https://www.theatlantic.com/business/archive/2012/10/did-katrina-victims-really-spend-their-r elief-money-on-gucci-bags-and-massage-parlors/264377/ (Retrieved Febrfuary 288, 2019).

28. Tejano music or Tex-Mex music describes several forms of folk and popular music among Mexican-American populations in Central and Southern Texas. Tejano became a popular music genre thanks to artists such as Selena, who was often referred to as "The Queen of Tejano."

29.Wikipedia defines a worldview as "the fundamental cognitive orientation of an individual or society encompassing the whole of the individual's or society's knowledge and point of view." That's the short version. For more, see https://en.wikipedia.org/wiki/World_view

30.Learn more about *food deserts* at https://socialwork.tulane.edu/blog/food-deserts-in-america.

31. "Childhood poverty is also associated with entrance into military service. Prior research indicates that individuals who experienced poverty and other ACEs in childhood are more likely to enroll in military service (at least in the all-volunteer era (Segal et al., 1998)), with Blosnich et al. (2014) hypothesizing 'that the military may serve as a route for a subset of persons to escape dysfunctional home environments, at least among men.' (p. E4)." Natalie Bareis and Briana Mezuk. "The Relationship Between Childhood Poverty, Military Service, and Later Life Depression among Men: Evidence from the Health and Retirement Study." National Center for Biotechnology Information, U.S. National Library of Medicine. https://www.ncbi.nlm.nih.gov/pmc/articles/PMC5704990/. (Retrieved February 28, 2019).

32. In His ministry, Jesus modeled this principle by finding and embracing "people of peace" wherever He went. See Luke 10:5-6, "Whatever house you enter, first say, 'Peace be to this house!' And if a son of peace is there, your peace will rest upon him. But if not, it will return to you."

33. In Texas, if a student lives within two miles of a school, the district is not required to offer bussing.

34. For a good summary of the McKinney-Vento Act of 1987 see https://communications.madison.k12.wi.us/files/pubinfo/McKinneyVentoAtAGlance.pdf.

35. It's called Reactive Attachment Disorder. While rare in general populations, Reactive Attachment Disorders can be diagnosed in up to 40% of people who experienced gross maltreatment or institutionalization as children. See: https://www.kidsnewtocanada.ca/mental-health/attachment-disorders

36. Our illustration of Broken Relations is adapted from When Helping Hurts

37. Ed Stetzer. "Avoiding The Pitfall of Syncretism." *Christianity Today*. https://www.christianitytoday.com/edstetzer/2014/june/avoiding-pitfall-of-syncretism.html. (Posted June 15, 2014)

38. Our illustration of Reconciliation is adapted from When Helping Hurts

39. Dr. King distilled this observation from an 1853 sermon by the Reverend Theodore Parker, "*I don't pretend to understand the moral universe. The arc is a long one. My eye reaches but little ways. I cannot calculate the curve and complete the figure by experience of sight. I can divine it by conscience. And from what I see I am sure it bends toward justice.*"

40. Robert Linthicum. *Building A People Of Power: Equipping Churches To Transform Their Communities.* (Authentic and World Vision, February 1, 2006).

41. Learn more about Step Up Ministries on their website at https://www.stepupministry.org/.

42. This tool is an adaptation of a tool originally found in Philip E. DeVol, Ruby K. Payne, and Terie Dreussi Smith. *Bridges Out of Poverty.* Revised edition 2009 (Highlands, TX: aha! Process, Inc., 2001).

www.ingramcontent.com/pod-product-compliance
Lightning Source LLC
Chambersburg PA
CBHW060041030426
42334CB00019B/2440